March 2011 — November 2011

AF861506

Review for the CFP® Exam

Volume 4: Income Tax Planning

KAPLAN SCHWESER

We value your input and suggestions. If you found imperfections in this product, please let us know by reporting it to Updates/Errata at www.schweser.com.

KAPLAN SCHWESER REVIEW FOR THE CFP® CERTIFICATION EXAMINATION
VOLUME 4: INCOME TAX PLANNING, MARCH 2011 THROUGH NOVEMBER 2011 EXAMS

Published by Kaplan Schweser.

Printed in the United States of America.

ISBN: 978-1-4277-2979-8 / 1-4277-2979-4
PPN: 3200-0578

10 11 10 09 08 07 06 05 04 03 02 01

Preface

PRODUCTS AND SERVICES FOR THE CFP® EXAM

KAPLAN SCHWESER REVIEW COURSES FOR THE CFP® EXAM

Kaplan Schweser offers several options to meet the diverse needs of candidates.

THE LIVE REVIEW COURSE

Instruction in both the traditional and virtual classroom programs consists mainly of teaching substantive material and helping students to master both the knowledge and application of topics that students will likely encounter on the exam. The course includes working through various types of problems to ensure that the substantive materials taught can be applied to exam-like questions. Students also receive instruction in actual exam-management techniques.

A video library of over 120 videos is available to Live Review students. These videos help students study important CFP® topics prior to the Live Review. Live Review students also have access to videos that walk them through cases in preparation for the CFP® Exam, as well as a video that replicates the CFP® Examination experience by working through a mock exam session.

Traditional Classroom Program

Kaplan Schweser offers the Traditional Classroom Program in major metropolitan areas across the country. The Four-Day Review is an intensive program consisting of over 30 hours of instruction conducted, in most cases, Thursday through Sunday.

The Virtual Classroom Program

Kaplan Schweser's Virtual Review is an instructor-led, web-based program that provides all the benefits of a classroom review from the convenience of the student's home or office. This program format is a great option for those who have access to the web and prefer not to incur the expense of travel. This course is an intensive program consisting of 33 hours of instruction in 11 three-hour classes. Students receive real-time interaction with the instructor and have access to a recorded playback option. Playbacks are also available for review until the first day of the CFP® Exam.

Live Review Study Tools

In-Class Student Guide

The In-Class Student Guide is an easy-to-use Live Review class companion with study notes to help keep students organized during and after class.

Diagnostic Exam

Available only to Live Review students, the Diagnostic Exam allows students to identify areas of strength and weakness prior to studying for the CFP® Exam. This study aid lets students tailor their study plans to the areas identified on a report that is provided once the Diagnostic Exam is completed.

Pre-Review Videos

Available on demand, pre-review videos provide instruction on exam topics that are not as challenging as topics covered during the Live Review, but for which students may still need to refresh.

Case Videos

As approximately 25% of the CFP® Exam's points are case-related, case preparation is critical. Students can master item sets and further develop their case analysis skills with this on-demand study tool.

Mock Exam Videos

Student can learn how to approach the CFP® Exam with this video that walks them through an exam simulation. Effective exam-taking techniques and advice are also offered.

Online Cognitive Connections QBank

These high-level, topic-integrated questions test students' comprehensive knowledge of the topics most likely covered on the CFP® Exam. Practice exams can be customized to students' areas of strengths and weaknesses.

VOLUMES 1–6

Volumes 1–6 contain complete reference outlines that give detailed coverage of each of the six tested areas of the CFP® Exam. Each volume contains examples, illustrations, and an index. Each volume has been updated to reflect 2011 law and inflation adjustments available at date of printing.

VOLUME 7—CASE BOOK

Volume 7—Case Book is designed to prepare students for the three comprehensive cases included on the exam. This valuable study tool provides the exam candidate with 16 comprehensive cases and item sets (minicases) that test students' knowledge and application of the exam topics. The answers and explanations for each multiple-choice question are provided, and the text has been updated to reflect 2011 law and inflation adjustments available at date of printing. Preparation in this area is extremely important as case questions are weighted more heavily than the general multiple-choice questions on the exam. Students who have used the *Case Book* have said that this book is a must to be prepared for the exam.

MOCK EXAM AND SOLUTIONS

Mock Exam and Solutions simulates the 10-hour comprehensive CFP® Examination. Similar to the actual exam, this online exam is divided into three sections, each containing multiple-choice questions, item sets, and a comprehensive case. This mock exam can serve as a diagnostic tool useful in identifying a student's areas of strength and weakness and can be used to help students focus on topics that they find more difficult. The mock exam is also updated to reflect 2011 law and inflation adjustments available at date of printing.

UNDERSTANDING YOUR FINANCIAL CALCULATOR

Understanding Your Financial Calculator is a book designed to assist students in gaining proficiency in using a financial calculator to work through problems they may encounter on the exam. In addition to helping master the keystrokes for the financial calculator, it is also designed to assist students with the underlying financial theory of these problems. All calculations are worked out step by step, showing keystrokes and displays for several of the most popular financial calculators.

Understanding Your Financial Calculator covers the basic operations of the calculators, basic time value of money calculations, fundamental problems (such as mortgages, education needs analysis, and retirement needs analysis), investment planning concepts, financial calculations (such as IRR, YTM, YTC, Sharpe, Treynor, Jensen, and standard deviation), and more. This text also includes a student practice section with over 200 basic, intermediate, and advanced practice problems and calculations. *Understanding Your Financial Calculator* is a great reference for the exam and for financial planning practitioners.

SCHWESERPRO™ ONLINE REVIEW QBANK

The SchweserPro™ online review QBank is an interactive software product of over 5,000 questions designed to give students practice in answering questions relating to content most likely tested on the CFP® Exam. Students can create customized, timed practice tests from the six topics tested on the CFP® Exam. All practice exams are scored and allow students to analyze their competency by topical areas. Customized tests may be saved for future reference.

ASSESSMENT EXAM

The Assessment Exam is an online tool designed to evaluate students' level of knowledge in the six topic areas covered on the CFP® Exam. Students can gauge the effectiveness of their learning at any point during the study process. Answers and rationales are provided at the end of the exam. A score report is also provided.

AUDIO REVIEWS

These audio reviews in mp3 format are designed as a general review of the six main topics covered on the CFP® Exam. Practice questions and solutions are also included.

CONTENT BLOGS

Students can learn more about the CFP® Exam and current topics of interest through short articles posted by subject matter experts. Students also have the ability to post responses to blogs and receive a reply from these experts.

INSTRUCTOR-LED OFFICE HOURS

Instructor guidance is also available to students through online real-time question and answer sessions, similar to instant messaging.

FREQUENTLY ASKED QUESTIONS (FAQs)

Questions frequently asked by students are presented in an online format, along with a detailed answer to each question. This serves as a valuable reference tool for students as they study for the exam.

FROM THE PUBLISHER

This text is intended as the basis for preparation for the CFP® Exam, either as self-study or as part of a review course. The material is organized according to the six functional areas tested on the exam and is presented in an outline format that includes examples and illustrations that help candidates quickly comprehend the material.

The material is organized into six manageable study units:

- Volume 1—*Fundamentals*
- Volume 2—*Insurance Planning*
- Volume 3—*Investments*
- Volume 4—*Income Tax Planning*
- Volume 5—*Retirement Planning*
- Volume 6—*Estate Planning*

We are indebted to Certified Financial Planner Board of Standards, Inc. for permission to reproduce and adapt their publications and other materials.

We welcome any comments concerning materials contained in or omitted from this text. Please submit your written comments to www.schweser.com.

Wishing you success on the exam,

Kaplan Schweser

CONTRIBUTING AUTHORS

- Kathy L. Berlin
  - —Senior Content Specialist, Kaplan Schweser
  - —Successfully passed CFP® Certification Examination
  - —Certified Public Accountant (Inactive)
  - —BA from Loyola University of New Orleans, Louisiana
  - —Former CFO of a large nonprofit organization
  - —Co-author of Kaplan Schweser's *Personal Financial Planning Cases and Applications, 5th – 7th Editions* textbook and instructor manual
  - —Co-author of Kaplan Schweser's *Personal Financial Planning Theory and Practice, 4th – 6th Editions* textbook and instructor manual
  - —Co-author of the *Schweser Review for the CFP® Certification Examination, 9th – 14th Editions*
- Glen Kramer, CRPC®, CFP®
  - —Senior Content Specialist, Kaplan Schweser
  - —BS in Economics from University of Wisconsin–Stevens Point
  - —Over 12 years of experience in the insurance and securities business
  - —Former General Securities Representative
  - —Former Life and Health Insurance Licensed Sales Representative in Arizona, Nevada, and Wisconsin
  - —Co-author of the *Schweser Review for the CFP® Certification Examination, 15th Edition*
- Michael Long, CLU®, ChFC®, CFP®
  - —Senior Content Specialist, Kaplan Schweser
  - —Over 25 years' experience in insurance and securities as a sales manager, classroom instructor, product manager, and advanced underwriting consultant
  - —BS in business administration, Indiana State University
  - —Co-author of Kaplan Schweser's *Personal Financial Planning Cases and Applications, 6th and 7th Editions* textbook and instructor manual
  - —Co-author of Kaplan Schweser's *Personal Financial Planning Theory and Practice, 6th Edition* textbook and instructor manual
  - —Co-author of the *Schweser Review for the CFP® Certification Examination, 13th and 14th Editions*
- James Maher, CLU®, ChFC®, CFP®
  - —Senior Content Specialist, Kaplan Schweser
  - —Former securities and insurance instructor, Kaplan Financial
  - —Former General Securities Representative
  - —BBA from Florida International University

—Co-author of Kaplan Schweser's *Personal Financial Planning Cases and Applications, 6th and 7th Editions* textbook and instructor manual

—Co-author of Kaplan Schweser's *Personal Financial Planning Theory and Practice, 5th and 6th Editions* textbook and instructor manual

—Co-author of the *Schweser Review for the CFP® Certification Examination, 12th – 14th Editions*

- Jeffrey B. Mershon, MBA, CPA/PFS, CFP®

  —Senior Content Specialist, Kaplan Schweser

  —Over 40 years public accounting, corporate finance and accounting, real estate, CFP Board, and financial planning education experience

  —BA in English Literature and MBA in Finance/Accounting, Cornell University

  —Author of Kaplan's *Fundamentals of Personal Financial Planning* and *Planning for Retirement* and co-author of *Insurance and Employee Benefits* and *Individual Income Tax Planning*

  —Co-author of Kaplan Schweser's *Personal Financial Planning Cases and Applications, 7th Edition* textbook and instructor manual

- Cindy R. Riecke, CLU®, ChFC®, CFP®

  —Senior Director, Kaplan Schweser

  —BS in Business Administration from Louisiana State University in Baton Rouge, Louisiana

  —Member of the Financial Planning Association

  —Former Director of Marketing Development for an international insurance and financial services company

  —Co-author of Kaplan Schweser's *Personal Financial Planning Cases and Applications, 5th – 7th Editions* textbook and instructor manual

  —Co-author of Kaplan Schweser's *Personal Financial Planning Theory and Practice, 4th – 6th Editions* textbook and instructor manual

  —Co-author of the *Schweser Review for the CFP® Certification Examination, 9th – 14th Editions*

- Stephan E. Wolter, JD, MBA, ChFC®

  —Senior Content Specialist, Kaplan Schweser

  —Successfully passed July 2008 CFP® Certification Examination

  —JD from Indiana University, Indianapolis

  —MBA from University of Colorado at Colorado Springs

  —Co-author of Kaplan Schweser's *Personal Financial Planning Cases and Applications, 6th and 7th Editions* textbook and instructor manual

  —Co-author of Kaplan Schweser's *Personal Financial Planning Theory and Practice, 6th Edition* textbook and instructor manual

  —Co-author of the *Schweser Review for the CFP® Certification Examination, 13th and 14th Editions*

ACKNOWLEDGMENTS AND SPECIAL THANKS

We are most appreciative of the tremendous support and encouragement we have received from everyone throughout this project, and are extremely grateful to the users of our texts who were gracious enough to provide us with valuable comments.

We very much appreciate the continued support of the many registered programs who have adopted our review materials. We understand that our success is a direct result of that support.

We greatly appreciate the assistance of Sharon Bonnem, who reviewed the Volumes 1 and 4 outlines for technical accuracy, and Marguerite Merritt, who reviewed the front matter and appendices for technical accuracy and assisted the subject-matter expert team with invaluable support.

We have received so much help from so many people, it is possible that we inadvertently overlooked thanking someone. If so, it is our shortcoming, and we apologize in advance. Please let us know if you are that someone, and we will correct it in our next printing.

We deeply appreciate the cooperation of CFP Board for granting us permission to reproduce and adapt their publications and other materials. CFP Board's Standards of Professional Conduct, copyrighted by CFP Board, is reprinted (or adapted) with permission.

Thanks to John J. Dardis for granting us permission to use material from "Estate & Benefit Planning Symposium" in *Volume 6—Estate Planning*.

Introduction

PURPOSE OF VOLUMES 1–6

Volumes 1–6 serve as the basis for preparation for the CFP® Exam either as self-study materials or as part of a review course. These volumes are organized by the six topic areas tested on the exam. Each volume presents its core content in outline format using examples, illustrations, and exhibits to help candidates quickly comprehend the material.

Volumes 1–6 cover the following topics:

- Volume 1—*Fundamentals*
- Volume 2—*Insurance Planning*
- Volume 3—*Investments*
- Volume 4—*Income Tax Planning*
- Volume 5—*Retirement Planning*
- Volume 6—*Estate Planning*

ABOUT THE CFP® EXAM

EXAMINATION PROCEDURES

Read carefully the procedures outlined in the *Guide to CFP® Certification*, available at www.cfp.net. The section entitled "CFP® Certification Examination" covers:

- dates of examinations;
- alternate test dates and test facilities;
- fees for the examination;
- scheduling confirmations;
- withdrawal from the exam;
- medical emergencies;
- items to bring to the examination;
- examination misconduct;
- examination scoring;
- score reports;
- pass score;
- reexamination procedures; and
- review and appeals.

A copy of the *Guide to CFP® Certification* also may be obtained from CFP Board, at the following address:

Certified Financial Planner Board of Standards, Inc.
1425 K Street, NW, Suite 500
Washington, DC 20005
Telephone: 1-800-487-1497
Fax: 1-202-379-2299
Website: www.cfp.net
Email: mail@CFPBoard.org

DATE GIVEN

The exam is generally given on the third Friday and Saturday of March, July, and November each year.

Friday (1 session—afternoon)	4 hours
Saturday (2 sessions)	6 hours
Total	10 hours

It is the student's responsibility to verify the exam and registration dates, as well as register for the exam.

For updates and information regarding the CFP® Exam, your exam registration, exam application deadlines, and so forth, please refer to CFP Board's Website at www.cfp.net.

For updates to Kaplan Schweser study materials (e.g., errata, legislative changes, and inflation-adjusted tax rate summaries), please refer to Updates/Errata at www.schweser.com.

QUESTION TYPES

The examination consists of approximately 285 multiple-choice questions. The majority of these are stand-alone questions that contain all relevant information within the body of the question. Also included are item set questions where one fact pattern will be used to answer several questions. A portion of the exam is in the form of case analysis. Each session of the exam contains one case with 15–20 questions. The information needed to answer these questions is generally found within the body of the case. These cases can be several pages long, making it difficult to efficiently organize the information to answer the questions.

The stand-alone questions, item sets, and case questions may test only one particular area of financial planning, such as investments. Many of the questions, however, are integrated questions, meaning that more than one topic is covered in the question. For example, a question might integrate investments and taxation. These integrated questions are designed to test your ability to analyze fact situations involving many planning considerations.

DISTRIBUTION OF TOPICS

The topics on the exam are targeted as follows:

Topic Covered	Percentage of the Exam
Fundamentals	11%
Insurance	14%
Investments	19%
Income tax	14%
Employee benefits*	8%
Retirement	19%
Estates	15%
Total	**100%**

*The majority of topics within the employee benefits section are discussed in the Insurance section. The remaining topics in employee benefits are discussed in the tax section. For an in-depth breakdown of all topics, please refer to the updated topic lists found later in this introduction.

Cognitive Levels Tested (Target)	Percentage of the Exam
Knowledge level	5%
Comprehension/application	35%
Analysis/synthesis/evaluation	60%
Total	**100%**

Scoring Method	Point Value per Question	Approximate Number	Points	Percentage
Stand-alone questions and item sets	2 points	235	470	76%
Case questions	3 points	50	150	24%
Total		**285**	**620**	**100%**

The examination division of CFP Board assigns the value weights to questions according to type, cognitive level, and level of difficulty.

TIME AND TIME ANALYSIS

There are 10 hours of examination time:

- Friday (4 hours)—1 case, item sets, and multiple choice
- Saturday (morning session, 3 hours)—1 case, item sets, and multiple choice
- Saturday (afternoon session, 3 hours)—1 case, item sets, and multiple choice
- Approximately 285 questions overall
- Case questions, average 15–20 per case

	Time (minutes)	Approximate Number of Multiple-Choice Questions	Average Time
Average indicated time per stand-alone and item set question	400	235	1.5–1.7 minutes each (Friday and Saturday)
Average indicated time per case question	200	50	4.0 minutes each (Friday and Saturday)
Average indicated time per question	600	285	2.1 minutes each (overall)

You should strive to average 1.5 minutes per question when practicing with online SchweserPro QBank questions. The cases and case analyses presented in *Volume 7: Case Book* should provide you with a realistic approximation of exam conditions regarding cases. The case multiple-choice questions should take about 75–90 minutes per set, including reading the case.

PASS RATES

The student pass rates have ranged from 50% to 63% on recent exams. This exam is a pass/fail professional exam with no partial credit. Therefore, it is vitally important that you be thoroughly prepared for all the topics covered on this examination.

KAPLAN SCHWESER'S PASS RATES

The Kaplan Schweser Live Reviews have consistently averaged a 70% to 80% first-time pass rate, which is 20% higher than the national average.

TOPIC LISTS FOR THE CFP® CERTIFICATION EXAMINATION

TOPIC LIST FOR CFP® CERTIFICATION EXAMINATION

The following topics, based on the 2004 Job Analysis Study, are the basis for the CFP® Certification Examinations. Each exam question will be linked to one of the following topics, in the approximate percentages indicated following the general headings. Questions will pertain to all levels in Bloom's taxonomy with an emphasis on the higher cognitive levels. Questions often will be asked in the context of the financial planning process and presented in an integrative format.

In addition to being used for the CFP® Certification Examination, this list indicates topic coverage requirements to fulfill the pre-certification educational requirement. Continuing education (CE) programs and materials that address these topics will be eligible for CFP Board CE credit.

(References to sections (§) in this list refer to sections of the Internal Revenue Code)

First Test Date: November 2006

GENERAL PRINCIPLES OF FINANCIAL PLANNING (11%)

1. Financial planning process
   A. Purpose, benefits, and components
   B. Steps
      1) Establishing client-planner relationships
      2) Gathering client data and determining goals and expectations
      3) Determining the client's financial status by analyzing and evaluating general financial status, special needs, insurance and risk management, investments, taxation, employee benefits, retirement, and/or estate planning
      4) Developing and presenting the financial plan
      5) Implementing the financial plan
      6) Monitoring the financial plan
   C. Responsibilities
      1) Financial planner
      2) Client
      3) Other advisors

2. CFP Board's *Code of Ethics and Professional Responsibility* and *Disciplinary Rules and Procedures*
   A. *Code of Ethics and Professional Responsibility*
      1) Preamble and applicability
      2) Composition and scope
      3) Compliance
      4) Terminology
      5) Principles
         a) Principle 1 - Integrity
         b) Principle 2 - Objectivity
         c) Principle 3 - Competence
         d) Principle 4 - Fairness
         e) Principle 5 - Confidentiality
         f) Principle 6 - Professionalism
         g) Principle 7 - Diligence
      6) Rules
   B) *Disciplinary Rules and Procedures*

3. CFP Board's *Financial Planning Practice Standards*
   A. Purpose and applicability
   B. Content of each series (use most current Practice Standards, as posted on CFP Board's Web site at www.CFP.net)
   C. Enforcement through *Disciplinary Rules and Procedures*

4. Financial statements
   A. Personal
      1) Statement of financial position
      2) Statement of cash flow
   B. Business
      1) Balance sheet
      2) Income statement
      3) Statement of cash flows
      4) Pro forma statements

5. Cash flow management
   A. Budgeting
   B. Emergency fund planning
   C. Debt management ratios
      1) Consumer debt
      2) Housing costs
      3) Total debt
   D. Savings strategies

6. Financing strategies
   A. Long-term vs. short-term debt
   B. Secured vs. unsecured debt
   C. Buy vs. lease/rent
   D. Mortgage financing
      1) Conventional vs. adjustable-rate mortgage (ARM)
      2) Home equity loan and line of credit
      3) Refinancing cost-benefit analysis
      4) Reverse mortgage

7. Function, purpose, and regulation of financial institutions
   A. Banks
   B. Credit unions
   C. Brokerage companies
   D. Insurance companies
   E. Mutual fund companies
   F. Trust companies

8. Education planning
   A. Funding
      1) Needs analysis
      2) Tax credits/adjustments/deductions
      3) Funding strategies
      4) Ownership of assets
      5) Vehicles
         a) Qualified tuition programs (§529 plans)
         b) Coverdell Education Savings Accounts
         c) Uniform Transfers to Minors Act (UTMA) and Uniform Gifts to Minors Act (UGMA) accounts
         d) Savings bonds
   B. Financial aid

9. Financial planning for special circumstances
   A. Divorce
   B. Disability
   C. Terminal illness
   D. Non-traditional families
   E. Job change and job loss
   F. Dependents with special needs
   G. Monetary windfalls

10. Economic concepts
    A. Supply and demand
    B. Fiscal policy
    C. Monetary policy
    D. Economic indicators
    E. Business cycles
    F. Inflation, deflation, and stagflation

Rev. 5/06

G. Yield curve

11. Time value of money concepts and calculations
    A. Present value
    B. Future value
    C. Ordinary annuity and annuity due
    D. Net present value (NPV)
    E. Internal rate of return (IRR)
    F. Uneven cash flows
    G. Serial payments

12. Financial services regulations and requirements
    A. Registration and licensing
    B. Reporting
    C. Compliance
    D. State securities and insurance laws

13. Business law
    A. Contracts
    B. Agency
    C. Fiduciary liability

14. Consumer protection laws
    A. Bankruptcy
    B. Fair credit reporting laws
    C. Privacy policies
    D. Identity theft protection

INSURANCE PLANNING AND RISK MANAGEMENT (14%)

15. Principles of risk and insurance
    A. Definitions
    B. Concepts
        1) Peril
        2) Hazard
        3) Law of large numbers
        4) Adverse selection
        5) Insurable risks
        6) Self-insurance
    C. Risk management process
    D. Response to risk
        1) Risk control
            a) Risk avoidance
            b) Risk diversification
            c) Risk reduction
        2) Risk financing
            a) Risk retention
            b) Risk transfer
    E. Legal aspects of insurance
        1) Principle of indemnity
        2) Insurable interest
        3) Contract requirements
        4) Contract characteristics
        5) Policy ownership
        6) Designation of beneficiary

16. Analysis and evaluation of risk exposures
    A. Personal
        1) Death
        2) Disability
        3) Poor health
        4) Unemployment
        5) Superannuation
    B. Property
        1) Real
        2) Personal
        3) Auto
    C. Liability
        1) Negligence
        2) Intentional torts
        3) Strict liability
    D. Business-related

17. Property, casualty and liability insurance
    A. Individual
        1) Homeowners insurance
        2) Auto insurance
        3) Umbrella liability insurance
    B. Business
        1) Commercial property insurance
        2) Commercial liability insurance
            a) Auto liability
            b) Umbrella liability
            c) Professional liability
            d) Directors and officers liability
            e) Workers' compensation and employers liability

18. Health insurance and health care cost management (individual)
    A. Hospital, surgical, and physicians' expense insurance
    B. Major medical insurance and calculation of benefits
    C. Continuance and portability
    D. Medicare
    E. Taxation of premiums and benefits

19. Disability income insurance (individual)
    A. Definitions of disability
    B. Benefit period
    C. Elimination period
    D. Benefit amount
    E. Provisions
    F. Taxation of premiums and benefits

20. Long-term care insurance (individual)
    A. Eligibility
    B. Services covered
    C. Medicare limitations
    D. Benefit period
    E. Elimination period
    F. Benefit amount
    G. Provisions
    H. Taxation of premiums and benefits

21. Life insurance (individual)
    A. Concepts and personal uses
    B. Policy types
    C. Contractual provisions
    D. Dividend options
    E. Nonforfeiture options
    F. Settlement options
    G. Illustrations
    H. Policy replacement
    I. Viatical and life settlements

22. Income taxation of life insurance
    A. Dividends
    B. Withdrawals and loans
    C. Death benefits
    D. Modified endowment contracts (MECs)
    E. Transfer-for-value
    F. §1035 exchanges

23. Business uses of insurance
    A. Buy-sell agreements
    B. Key employee life insurance
    C. Split-dollar life insurance
    D. Business overhead expense insurance

24. Insurance needs analysis
    A. Life insurance
    B. Disability income insurance
    C. Long-term care insurance
    D. Health insurance
    E. Property insurance
    F. Liability insurance

25. Insurance policy and company selection
    A. Purpose of coverage
    B. Duration of coverage
    C. Participating or non-participating
    D. Cost-benefit analysis
    E. Company selection
        1) Industry ratings
        2) Underwriting

26. Annuities
    A. Types
    B. Uses
    C. Taxation

EMPLOYEE BENEFITS PLANNING (8%)

27. Group life insurance
    A. Types and basic provisions
        1) Group term
        2) Group permanent
        3) Dependent coverage
    B. Income tax implications
    C. Employee benefit analysis and application
    D. Conversion analysis

28. Group disability insurance
    A. Types and basic provisions
        1) Short-term coverage
        2) Long-term coverage
    B. Definitions of disability
    C. Income tax implications
    D. Employee benefit analysis and application
    E. Integration with other income

Rev. 5/06

29. Group medical insurance
    A. Types and basic provisions
        1) Traditional indemnity
        2) Managed care plans
            a) Preferred provider organization (PPO)
            b) Health maintenance organization (HMO)
            c) Point-of-service (POS)
    B. Income tax implications
    C. Employee benefit analysis and application
    D. COBRA/HIPAA provisions
    E. Continuation
    F. Savings accounts
        1) Health savings account (HSA)
        2) Archer medical savings account (MSA)
        3) Health reimbursement arrangement (HRA)

30. Other employee benefits
    A. §125 cafeteria plans and flexible spending accounts (FSAs)
    B. Fringe benefits
    C. Voluntary employees' beneficiary association (VEBA)
    D. Prepaid legal services
    E. Group long-term care insurance
    F. Dental insurance
    G. Vision insurance

31. Employee stock options
    A. Basic provisions
        1) Company restrictions
        2) Transferability
        3) Exercise price
        4) Vesting
        5) Expiration
        6) Cashless exercise
    B. Incentive stock options (ISOs)
        1) Income tax implications (regular, AMT, basis)
            a) Upon grant
            b) Upon exercise
            c) Upon sale
        2) Holding period requirements
        3) Disqualifying dispositions
        4) Planning opportunities and strategies
    C. Non-qualified stock options (NSOs)
        1) Income tax implications (regular, AMT, basis)
            a) Upon grant
            b) Upon exercise
            c) Upon sale
        2) Gifting opportunities
            a) Unvested/vested
            b) Exercised/unexercised
            c) Gift tax valuation
            d) Payment of gift tax
        3) Planning opportunities and strategies
        4) Employee benefits analysis and application
    D. Planning strategies for employees with both incentive stock options and non-qualified stock options
    E. Election to include in gross income in the year of transfer (§83(b) election)

32. Stock plans
    A. Types and basic provisions
        1) Restricted stock
        2) Phantom stock
        3) Stock appreciation rights(SARs)
        4) Employee stock purchase plan (ESPP)
    B. Income tax implications
    C. Employee benefit analysis and application
    D. Election to include in gross income in the year of transfer (§83(b) election)

33. Non-qualified deferred compensation
    A. Basic provisions and differences from qualified plans
    B. Types of plans and applications
        1) Salary reduction plans
        2) Salary continuation plans
        3) Rabbi trusts
        4) Secular trusts
    C. Income tax implications
        1) Constructive receipt
        2) Substantial risk of forfeiture
        3) Economic benefit doctrine
    D. Funding methods
    E. Strategies

INVESTMENT PLANNING (19%)

34. Characteristics, uses and taxation of investment vehicles
    A. Cash and equivalents
        1) Certificates of deposit
        2) Money market funds
        3) Treasury bills
        4) Commercial paper
        5) Banker's acceptances
        6) Eurodollars
    B. Individual bonds
        1) U.S. Government bonds and agency securities
            a) Treasury notes and bonds
            b) Treasury STRIPS
            c) Treasury inflation-protection securities (TIPS)
            d) Series EE, HH, and I bonds
            e) Mortgage-backed securities
        2) Zero-coupon bonds
        3) Municipal bonds
            a) General obligation
            b) Revenue
        4) Corporate bonds
            a) Mortgage bond
            b) Debenture
            c) Investment grade
            d) High-yield
            e) Convertible
            f) Callable
        5) Foreign bonds
    C. Promissory notes
    D. Individual stocks
        1) Common
        2) Preferred
        3) American depositary receipts (ADRs)
    E. Pooled and managed investments
        1) Exchange-traded funds (ETFs)
        2) Unit investment trusts
        3) Mutual funds
        4) Closed-end investment companies
        5) Index securities
        6) Hedge funds
        7) Limited partnerships
        8) Privately managed accounts
        9) Separately managed accounts
    F. Guaranteed investmentcontracts (GICs)
    G. Real Estate
        1) Investor-managed
        2) Real estate investment trusts (REITs)
        3) Real estate limited partnerships (RELPs)
        4) Real estate mortgage investment conduits (REMICs)
    H. Alternative investments
        1) Derivatives
            a) Puts
            b) Calls
            c) Long-term Equity AnticiPation Securities (LEAPS®)
            d) Futures
            e) Warrants and rights
        2) Tangible assets
            a) Collectibles
            b) Natural resources
            c) Precious metals

35. Types of investment risk
    A. Systematic/market/nondiversifiable
    B. Purchasing power
    C. Interest rate
    D. Unsystematic/nonmarket/diversifiable
    E. Business
    F. Financial
    G. Liquidity and marketability
    H. Reinvestment
    I. Political (sovereign)
    J. Exchange rate
    K. Tax
    L. Investment manager

36. Quantitative investment concepts
    A. Distribution of returns
        1) Normal distribution
        2) Lognormal distribution
        3) Skewness
        4) Kurtosis

Rev. 5/06

- B. Correlation coefficient
- C. Coefficient of determination (R2)
- D. Coefficient of variation
- E. Standard deviation
- F. Beta
- G. Covariance
- H. Semivariance

37. Measures of investment returns
    - A. Simple vs. compound return
    - B. Geometric average vs. arithmeticaverage return
    - C. Time-weighted vs. dollar-weighted return
    - D. Real (inflation-adjusted) vs. nominal return
    - E. Total return
    - F. Risk-adjusted return
    - G. Holding period return
    - H. Internal rate of return (IRR)
    - I. Yield-to-maturity
    - J. Yield-to-call
    - K. Current yield
    - L. Taxable equivalent yield (TEY)

38. Bond and stock valuation concepts
    - A. Bond duration and convexity
    - B. Capitalized earnings
    - C. Dividend growth models
    - D. Ratio analysis
        - 1) Price/earnings
        - 2) Price/free cash flow
        - 3) Price/sales
        - 4) Price/earnings ÷ growth (PEG)
    - E. Book value

39. Investment theory
    - A. Modern portfolio theory (MPT)
        - 1) Capital market line (CML)
            - a) Mean-variance optimization
            - b) Efficient frontier
        - 2) Security market line (SML)
    - B. Efficient market hypothesis (EMH)
        - 1) Strong form
        - 2) Semi-strong form
        - 3) Weak form
        - 4) Anomalies
    - C. Behavioral finance

40. Portfolio development and analysis
    - A. Fundamental analysis
        - 1) Top-down analysis
        - 2) Bottom-up analysis
        - 3) Ratio analysis
            - a) Liquidity ratios
            - b) Activity ratios
            - c) Profitability ratios
            - d) Debt ratios
    - B. Technical analysis
        - 1) Charting
        - 2) Sentiment indicators
        - 3) Flow of funds indicators
        - 4) Market structure indicators
    - C. Investment policy statements
    - D. Appropriate benchmarks
    - E. Probability analysis, includingMonte Carlo
    - F. Tax efficiency
        - 1) Turnover
        - 2) Timing of capital gains and losses
        - 3) Wash sale rule
        - 4) Qualified dividends
        - 5) Tax-free income
    - G. Performance measures
        - 1) Sharpe ratio
        - 2) Treynor ratio
        - 3) Jensen ratio
        - 4) Information ratio

41. Investment strategies
    - A. Market timing
    - B. Passive investing (indexing)
    - C. Buy and hold
    - D. Portfolio immunization
    - E. Swaps and collars
    - F. Formula investing
        - 1) Dollar cost averaging
        - 2) Dividend reinvestment plans (DRIPs)
        - 3) Bond ladders, bullets, and barbells
    - G. Use of leverage (margin)
    - H. Short selling
    - I. Hedging and option strategies

42. Asset allocation and portfolio diversification
    - A. Strategic asset allocation
        - 1) Application of client lifecycle analysis
        - 2) Client risk tolerance measurement and application
        - 3) Asset class definition and correlation
    - B. Rebalancing
    - C. Tactical asset allocation
    - D. Control of volatility
    - E. Strategies for dealing with concentrated portfolios

43. Asset pricing models
    - A. Capital asset pricing model (CAPM)
    - B. Arbitrage pricing theory (APT)
    - C. Black-Scholes option valuation model
    - D. Binomial option pricing

INCOME TAX PLANNING (14%)

44. Income tax law fundamentals
    - A. Types of authority
        - 1) Primary
        - 2) Secondary
    - B. Research sources

45. Tax compliance
    - A. Filing requirements
    - B. Audits
    - C. Penalties

46. Income tax fundamentals and calculations
    - A. Filing status
    - B. Gross income
        - 1) Inclusions
        - 2) Exclusions
        - 3) Imputed income
    - C. Adjustments
    - D. Standard/Itemized deductions
        - 1) Types
        - 2) Limitations
    - E. Personal and dependency exemptions
    - F. Taxable income
    - G. Tax liability
        - 1) Rate schedule
        - 2) Kiddie tax
        - 3) Self-employment tax
    - H. Tax credits
    - I. Payment of tax
        - 1) Withholding
        - 2) Estimated payments

47. Tax accounting
    - A. Accounting periods
    - B. Accounting methods
        - 1) Cash receipts and disbursements
        - 2) Accrual method
        - 3) Hybrid method
        - 4) Change in accounting method
    - C. Long-term contracts
    - D. Installment sales
    - E. Inventory valuation and flow methods
    - F. Net operating losses

48. Characteristics and income taxation of business entities
    - A. Entity types
        - 1) Sole proprietorship
        - 2) Partnerships
        - 3) Limited liability company (LLC)
        - 4) Corporations
        - 5) Trust
        - 6) Association
    - B. Taxation at entity and owner level
        - 1) Formation
        - 2) Flow through of income and losses
        - 3) Special taxes
        - 4) Distributions
        - 5) Dissolution
        - 6) Disposition

49. Income taxation of trusts and estates
    - A. General issues
        - 1) Filing requirements
        - 2) Deadlines
        - 3) Choice of taxable year

Rev. 5/06

4) Tax treatment of distributions to beneficiaries
5) Rate structure
B. Grantor/Nongrantor trusts
C. Simple/Complex trusts
D. Revocable/Irrevocable trusts
E. Trust income
1) Trust accounting income
2) Trust taxable income
3) Distributable net income (DNI)
F. Estate income tax

50. Basis
A. Original basis
B. Adjusted basis
C. Amortization and accretion
D. Basis of property received by gift and in nontaxable transactions
E. Basis of inherited property (community and non-community property)

51. Depreciation/cost-recovery concepts
A. Modified Accelerated Cost Recovery System (MACRS)
B. Expensing policy
C. §179 deduction
D. Amortization
E. Depletion

52. Tax consequences of like-kind exchanges
A. Reporting requirements
B. Qualifying transactions
C. Liabilities
D. Boot
E. Related party transactions

53. Tax consequences of the disposition of property
A. Capital assets (§1221)
B. Holding period
C. Sale of residence
D. Depreciation recapture
E. Related parties
F. Wash sales
G. Bargain sales
H. Section 1244 stock (small business stock election)
I. Installment sales
J. Involuntary conversions

54. Alternative minimum tax (AMT)
A. Mechanics
B. Preferences and adjustments
C. Exclusion items vs. deferral items
D. Credit:creation, usage, and limitations
E. Application to businesses and trusts
F. Planning strategies

55. Tax reduction/management techniques
A. Tax credits
B. Accelerated deductions
C. Deferral of income
D. Intra-family transfers

56. Passive activity and at-risk rules
A. Definitions
B. Computations
C. Treatment of disallowed losses
D. Disposition of passive activities
E. Real estate exceptions

57. Tax implications of special circumstances
A. Married/widowed
1) Filing status
2) Children
3) Community and non-community property
B. Divorce
1) Alimony
2) Child support
3) Property division

58. Charitable contributions and deductions
A. Qualified entities
1) Public charities
2) Private charities
B. Deduction limitations
C. Carryover periods
D. Appreciated property
E. Non-deductible contributions
F. Appraisals
G. Substantiation requirements
H. Charitable contributions by business entities

RETIREMENT PLANNING (19%)

59. Retirement needs analysis
A. Assumptions for retirement planning
1) Inflation
2) Retirement period and life expectancy
3) Lifestyle
4) Total return
B. Income sources
C. Financial needs
1) Living costs
2) Charitable and beneficiary gifting objectives
3) Medical costs, including long-term care needs analysis
4) Other (trust and foundation funding, education funding, etc.)
D. Straight-line returns vs. probability analysis
E. Pure annuity vs. capital preservation
F. Alternatives to compensate for projected cash-flow shortfalls

60. Social Security (Old Age, Survivor, and Disability Insurance, OASDI)
A. Paying into the system
B. Eligibility and benefit
1) Retirement
2) Disability
3) Survivor
4) Family limitations
C. How benefits are calculated
D. Working after retirement
E. Taxation of benefits

61. Types of retirement plans
A. Characteristics
1) Qualified plans
2) Non-qualified plans
B. Types and basic provisions of qualified plans
1) Defined contribution
a) Money purchase
b) Target benefit
c) Profit sharing
1) 401(k) plan
2) Safe harbor 401(k) plan
3) Age-based plan
4) Stock bonus plan
5) Employee stock ownership plan (ESOP)
6) New comparability plan
7) Thrift plan
2) Defined benefit
a) Traditional
b) Cash balance
c) 412(i) plan

62. Qualified plan rules and options
A. Nondiscrimination and eligibility requirements
1) Age and service requirements
2) Coverage requirements
3) Minimum participation
4) Highly compensated employee (HCE)
5) Permitted vesting schedules
6) ADP/ACP testing
7) Controlled group
B. Integration with Social Security/disparity limits
1) Defined benefit plans
2) Defined contribution plans
C. Factors affecting contributions or benefits
1) Deduction limit (§404(c))
2) Defined contribution limits
3) Defined benefit limit
4) Annual compensation limit
5) Definition of compensation
6) Multiple plans
7) Special rules for self-employed (non-corporations)
D. Top-heavy plans
1) Definition
2) Key employee
3) Vesting
4) Effects on contributions or benefits
E. Loans from qualified plans

Rev. 5/06

63. Other tax-advantaged retirement plans
    A. Types and basic provisions
        1) Traditional IRA
        2) Roth IRA, including conversion analysis
        3) SEP
        4) SIMPLE
        5) §403(b) plans
        6) §457 plans
        7) Keogh (HR-10) plans

64. Regulatory considerations
    A. Employee Retirement Income Security Act (ERISA)
    B. Department of Labor (DOL) regulations
    C. Fiduciary liability issues
    D. Prohibited transactions
    E. Reporting requirements

65. Key factors affecting plan selection for businesses
    A. Owner's personal objectives
        1) Tax considerations
        2) Capital needs at retirement
        3) Capital needs at death
    B. Business' objectives
        1) Tax considerations
        2) Administrative cost
        3) Cash flow situation and outlook
        4) Employee demographics
        5) Comparison of defined contribution and defined benefit plan alternatives

66. Investment considerations for retirement plans
    A. Suitability
    B. Time horizon
    C. Diversification
    D. Fiduciary considerations
    E. Unrelated business taxable income (UBTI)
    F. Life insurance
    G. Appropriate assets for tax-advantaged vs. taxable accounts

67. Distribution rules, alternatives,and taxation
    A. Premature distributions
        1) Penalties
        2) Exceptions to penalties
        3) Substantially equal payments (§72(t))
    B. Election of distribution options
        1) Lump sum distributions
        2) Annuity options
        3) Rollover
        4) Direct transfer
    C. Required minimum distributions
        1) Rules
        2) Calculations
        3) Penalties
    D. Beneficiary considerations/Stretch IRAs
    E. Qualified domestic relations order (QDRO)
    F. Taxation of distributions
        1) Tax management techniques
        2) Net unrealized appreciation (NUA)

ESTATE PLANNING (15%)

68. Characteristics and consequences of property titling
    A. Community property vs. non-community property
    B. Sole ownership
    C. Joint tenancy with right of survivorship (JTWROS)
    D. Tenancy by the entirety
    E. Tenancy in common
    F. Trust ownership

69. Methods of property transfer at death
    A. Transfers through the probate process
        1) Testamentary distribution
        2) Intestate succession
        3) Advantages and disadvantages of probate
        4) Assets subject to probate estate
        5) Probate avoidance strategies
        6) Ancillary probate administration
    B. Transfers by operation of law
    C. Transfers through trusts
    D. Transfers by contract

70. Estate planning documents
    A. Wills
        1) Legal requirements
        2) Types of wills
        3) Modifying or revoking a will
        4) Avoiding will contests
    B. Powers of Attorney
    C. Trusts
    D. Marital property agreements
    E. Buy-sell agreements

71. Gifting strategies
    A. Inter-vivos gifting
    B. Gift-giving techniques and strategies
    C. Appropriate gift property
    D. Strategies for closely-held business owners
    E. Gifts of present and future interests
    F. Gifts to non-citizen spouses
    G. Tax implications
        1) Income
        2) Gift
        3) Estate
        4) Generation-skipping transfer tax (GSTT)

72. Gift tax compliance and tax calculation
    A. Gift tax filing requirements
    B. Calculation
        1) Annual exclusion
        2) Applicable credit amount
        3) Gift splitting
        4) Prior taxable gifts
        5) Education and medical exclusions
        6) Marital and charitable deductions
        7) Tax liability

73. Incapacity planning
    A. Definition of incapacity
    B. Powers of attorney
        1) For health care decisions
        2) For asset management
        3) Durable feature
        4) Springing power
        5) General or limited powers
    C. Advance medical directives (e.g. living wills)
    D. Guardianship and conservatorship
    E. Revocable living trust
    F. Medicaid planning
    G. Special needs trust

74. Estate tax compliance and tax calculation
    A. Estate tax filing requirements
    B. The gross estate
        1) Inclusions
        2) Exclusions
    C. Deductions
    D. Adjusted gross estate
    E. Deductions from the adjusted gross estate
    F. Taxable estate
    G. Adjusted taxable gifts
    H. Tentative tax base
    I. Tentative tax calculation
    J. Credits
        1) Gift tax payable
        2) Applicable credit amount
        3) Prior transfer credit

75. Sources for estate liquidity
    A. Sale of assets
    B. Life insurance
    C. Loan

76. Powers of appointment
    A. Use and purpose
    B. General and special (limited) powers
        1) 5-and-5 power
        2) Crummey powers
        3) Distributions for an ascertainable standard
        4) Lapse of power
    C. Tax implications

77. Types, features, and taxation of trusts
    A. Classification
        1) Simple and complex
        2) Revocable and irrevocable
        3) Inter-vivos and testamentary

Rev. 5/06

B. Types and basic provisions
   1) Totten trust
   2) Spendthrift trust
   3) Bypass trust
   4) Marital trust
   5) Qualified terminable interest property (QTIP) trust
   6) Pour-over trust
   7) §2503(b) trust
   8) §2503(c) trust
   9) Sprinkling provision
C. Trust beneficiaries: Income and remainder
D. Rule against perpetuities
E. Estate and gift taxation

78. Qualified interest trusts
   A. Grantor retained annuity trusts (GRATs)
   B. Grantor retained unitrusts (GRUTs)
   C. Qualified personal residence trusts (QPRTs or House-GRITs)
   D. Valuation of qualified interests

79. Charitable transfers
   A. Outright gifts
   B. Charitable remainder trusts
      1) Unitrusts (CRUTs)
      2) Annuity trusts(CRATs)
   C. Charitable lead trusts
      1) Unitrusts (CLUTs)
      2) Annuity trusts (CLATs)
   D. Charitable gift annuities
   E. Pooled income funds
   F. Private foundations
   G. Donor advised funds
   H. Estate and gift taxation

80. Use of life insurance in estate planning
   A. Incidents of ownership
   B. Ownership and beneficiary considerations
   C. Irrevocable life insurance trust (ILIT)
   D. Estate and gift taxation

81. Valuation issues
   A. Estate freezes
      1) Corporate and partnership recapitalizations (§2701)
      2) Transfers in trust
   B. Valuation discounts for business interests
      1) Minority discounts
      2) Marketability discounts
      3) Blockage discounts
      4) Key person discounts
   C. Valuation techniques and thefederal gross estate

82. Marital deduction
   A. Requirements
   B. Qualifying transfers
   C. Terminable interest rule and exceptions
   D. Qualified domestic trust (QDOT)

83. Deferral and minimization of estate taxes
   A. Exclusion of property from the gross estate
   B. Lifetime gifting strategies
   C. Marital deduction and bypass trust planning
   D. Inter-vivos and testamentary charitable gifts

84. Intra-family and other business transfer techniques
   A. Characteristics
   B. Techniques
      1) Buy-sell agreement
      2) Installment note
      3) Self-canceling installment note (SCIN)
      4) Private annuity
      5) Transfers in trust
      6) Intra-family loan
      7) Bargain sale
      8) Gift or sale leaseback
      9) Intentionally defective grantor trust
      10) Family limited partnership (FLP) or limited liability company (LLC)
   C. Federal income, gift, estate, and generation-skipping transfer tax implications

85. Generation-skipping transfer tax (GSTT)
   A. Identify transfers subject to the GSTT
      1) Direct skips
      2) Taxable distributions
      3) Taxable terminations
   B. Exemptions and exclusions from the GSTT
      1) The GSTT exemption
      2) Qualifying annual exclusion gifts and direct transfers

86. Fiduciaries
   A. Types of fiduciaries
      1) Executor/Personal representative
      2) Trustee
      3) Guardian
   B. Duties of fiduciaries
   C. Breach of fiduciary duties

87. Income in respect of a decedent (IRD)
   A. Assets qualifying as IRD
   B. Calculation for IRD deduction
   C. Income tax treatment

88. Postmortem estate planning techniques
   A. Alternate valuation date
   B. Qualified disclaimer
   C. Deferral of estate tax (§6166)
   D. Corporate stock redemption (§303)
   E. Special use valuation (§2032A)

89. Estate planning for non-traditional relationships
   A. Children of another relationship
   B. Cohabitation
   C. Adoption
   D. Same-sex relationships

ADDENDUM

The following topics are an addendum to the Topic List for CFP® Certification Examination. Although individuals taking the CFP® Certification Examination will not be tested directly over these topics, CFP Board-Registered Programs are strongly encouraged to teach them in their curricula. Continuing education (CE) programs and materials that address these topics will be eligible for CFP Board CE credit.

1. Client and planner attitudes, values, biases and behavioral characteristics and the impact on financial planning
   - A. Cultural
   - B. Family (e.g. biological; non-traditional)
   - C. Emotional
   - D. Life cycle and age
   - E. Client's level of knowledge, experience, and expertise
   - F. Risk tolerance
   - G. Values-driven planning
2. Principles of communication and counseling
   - A. Types of structured communication
     - 1) Interviewing
     - 2) Counseling
     - 3) Advising
   - B. Essentials in financial counseling
     - 1) Establishing structure
     - 2) Creating rapport
     - 3) Recognizing resistance
   - C. Characteristics of effective counselors
     - 1) Unconditional positive regard
     - 2) Accurate empathy
     - 3) Genuineness and self-awareness
   - D. Nonverbal behaviors
     - 1) Body positions, movements, and gestures
     - 2) Facial expressions and eye contact
     - 3) Voice tone and pitch
     - 4) Interpreting the meaning of nonverbal behaviors
   - E. Attending and listening skills
     - 1) Physical attending
     - 2) Active listening
     - 3) Responding during active listening; leading responses
   - F. Effective use of questions
     - 1) Appropriate types of questions
     - 2) Ineffective and counterproductive questioning techniques

Rev. 5/06

Table of Contents

TABLE OF EXHIBITS

TABLE OF APPENDICES

Income Tax Planning

I. TAX LAW—LEGISLATIVE, ADMINISTRATIVE, AND JUDICIAL

A. LEGISLATIVE SOURCES OF THE TAX LAW

1. The Internal Revenue Code (IRC)
   a. The Internal Revenue Code is the highest source of tax authority
   b. In 1939, Congress codified (combined and organized) the federal tax laws. The IRC was recodified in 1954. The Tax Reform Act of 1986 (TRA) renamed the 1954 code the Internal Revenue Code of 1986.
   c. The IRC is located in Title 26, and income taxes are located in Subtitle A. The IRC is normally quoted by code sections, which are typically broken down into subparts. For example, Section 150(e)(1)(A) cites Section 150, subsection (e), paragraph (1), and subparagraph (A).
2. Objective of treaties—the United States is a partner to over 40 income tax treaties with other countries. The primary purpose of these treaties is to establish primary taxing authority. When treaties conflict with the IRC, the Technical and Miscellaneous Revenue Act of 1988 provides that the most recent treaty prevails.

B. EXECUTIVE SOURCES OF THE TAX LAW

1. Treasury Department Regulations—the highest source of authority next to the Code. Regulations have the full force and effect of the law.
   a. Provides the official interpretation of the Tax Code by the Treasury Department
2. The Internal Revenue Bulletin (IRB)—announces official rulings and procedures of the IRS and publishes Treasury Decisions, Executive Orders, Tax Conventions, legislation, court decisions, and other items of general interest
   a. Rulings and procedures reported in the IRB do not have the force and effect of Treasury tax regulations, but they may be used as precedents
   b. In contrast, any documents not published in the IRB cannot be relied on, used, or cited as precedents in the disposition of other cases
3. Revenue Rulings—provide interpretations of the tax law with regard to taxable income, deductions, and credits
   a. Do not have the full force of law and do not carry the force and effect of regulations but can be cited as precedent
   b. Are published by the government to give guidance to IRS personnel and taxpayers
   c. The number system contains the year in which the ruling was issued and the order it was released: Revenue Ruling 2010-4 was the fourth Revenue Ruling published in 2010

c. The Bureau of National Affairs, Inc. (BNA)
   1.) Publishes Income Tax Portfolios, which is a multivolume set with periodic updates
   2.) Includes lengthy explanatory text for the IRC and regulations
   3.) Organized by topic, with a separate portfolio for each topic

2. Periodicals
   a. Tax newsletters and magazines
      1.) *Taxes—The Tax Magazine*
      2.) *Tax Notes*
      3.) *Journal of Taxation*
      4.) *BNA Daily Tax Report*
      5.) *BNA Financial Planning Journal*
   b. Tax Internet services
      1.) CCH Tax Research Network
      2.) Leimberg Information Services
      3.) *LawThreads*™
      4.) IRS Website
      5.) *RIA Checkpoint*

II. TAX RATES AND BRACKETS

A. RATES AND BRACKETS

1. The following exhibit represents the 2011 tax rates and brackets
   a. Exhibit 3 includes the projected tax rates and abbreviated brackets that may be effective in 2011 due to the EGTRRA sunset, and were available at date of printing. For tax rates and brackets that may be amended by Congress subsequently, please go to the Errata and Updates page of our website.

EXHIBIT 3: 2011 Tax Rates and Brackets (Under EGTRRA Sunset Rules)

Single—Schedule X		
If taxable income is over:	But not over:	The tax rate is:
$0	$34,500	15%
$34,500	$83,600	28%
$83,600	$174,400	31%
$174,400	$379,150	36%
$379,150	------------	39.6%

Head of Household—Schedule Z		
If taxable income is over:	But not over:	The tax rate is:
$0	$46,250	15%
$46,250	$119,400	28%
$119,400	$193,350	31%
$193,350	$379,150	36%
$379,150	------------	39.6%

Married Filing Jointly or Qualifying Widow(er)—Schedule Y-1		
If taxable income is over:	But not over:	The tax rate is:
$0	$57,650	15%
$57,650	$139,350	28%
$139,350	$212,300	31%
$212,300	$379,150	36%
$379,150	------------	39.6%

Married Filing Separately—Schedule Y-2		
If taxable income is over:	But not over:	The tax rate is:
$0	$28,825	15%
$28,825	$69,675	28%
$69,675	$106,150	31%
$106,150	$189,575	36%
$189,575	------------	39.6%

Estates and Trusts		
If taxable income is:	But not over:	The tax rate is:
$0	$2,300	------- 15%
$2,300	$5,450	28%
$5,450	$8,300	31%
$8,300	$11,350	36%
$11,350	------------	39.6%

III. BASIC TAX FORMULA AND INFLATION-ADJUSTED AMOUNTS

A. THE TAX FORMULA

Income (broadly conceived)	$xx,xxx	*Section IV. Gross Income Inclusions*
Less exclusions from gross income	(x,xxx)	*Section V. Gross Income—Exclusions*
Gross income	$xx,xxx	
Less deductions for adjusted gross income (AGI)	(x,xxx)	*Section VI. Deductions for Adjusted Gross Income*
AGI	$xx,xxx	
Less the greater of:		
Total itemized deductions or standard deduction	(x,xxx)	*Section VII. Basic Standard Deduction and Additional Standard Deductions*
Less personal and dependency exemptions	(x,xxx)	*Section VIII. Personal and Dependency Exemptions*
Taxable income	$xx,xxx	

B. REQUIRED TAX PAYMENTS

1. Employers must withhold income taxes and FICA (Social Security and Medicare) taxes from their employees' paychecks
   a. Withholding is deemed to be paid throughout the year regardless of when it is actually withheld
2. Taxpayers who receive income that is not subject to withholding must make quarterly estimated tax payments
   a. For calendar-year taxpayers, estimated payment due dates are April 15, June 15, September 15, and January 15 of the following year. If the 15th falls on a Saturday or Sunday, the due date will be the following Monday.
   b. To avoid an underpayment penalty, taxpayers must make estimated payments that are the lesser of:
      1.) 90% of the tax liability shown on the current year return;
      2.) 100% of tax liability shown on prior year return if AGI is $150,000 or less; or
      3.) if AGI is greater than $150,000, 110% of the prior year's tax liability
3. No penalty is imposed if the taxpayer did not have a tax liability for the previous yea

B. ACCOUNTING PERIODS

1. In general
   a. Taxable income is generally computed on the basis of an annual accounting period, known as a taxable year
   b. A taxable year is the annual period over which income is measured for income tax purposes
   c. A calendar year is a 12-month period ending on December 31. Most individuals and many businesses use the calendar year.
   d. A fiscal year is a 12-month period ending on the last day of any month other than December
      1.) May use a fiscal year based on the natural business year (e.g., a school may have a fiscal year that begins August 1 and ends July 31)
2. Requirements
   a. All taxpayers may use a calendar year
   b. A fiscal year may be adopted only by taxpayers who maintain adequate records
   c. The accounting period is established when an individual or business files its initial income tax return
      1.) Once established, the taxpayer can change it only with IRS consent
3. Tax year for business entities
   a. Partnerships generally must use the same tax year as the tax year of the partners, unless the partnership can establish a business purpose for having a different tax year
   b. S corporations generally must use the calendar year, unless the S corporation can establish a business purpose for having a different tax year
      1.) If a partner or S corporation shareholder has a different tax year than the partnership or S corporation, the partner or shareholder must report his share of the entity's income in the taxable year within which the entity's tax year ends

> **EXAMPLE** Orentlich Partners is a partnership with a fiscal year ending on September 30. Bethany, a 20% partner in the partnership, is a calendar year individual taxpayer. For the taxable year ending September 30, 2010, Orentlich had operating income of $100,000. Orentlich also had operating income of $30,000 for the period of October 1, 2010, through December 31, 2010. Bethany must report $20,000 (20% partnership interest × $100,000 partnership income) on her year 2010 income tax return. Any income earned by the partnership from October 2010 through December 2010 will be reported on Bethany's 2011 tax return.

C. ACCOUNTING METHODS

1. Cash method
   a. Income is reported when cash is collected (or taxpayer has constructive receipt) and expenses are reported when cash payments are made

b. For fixed assets (e.g., equipment), a deduction is claimed through depreciation in the same manner as an accrual-basis taxpayer

c. Prepaid expenses must be capitalized and amortized if the life of the asset extends substantially beyond the end of the tax year

d. The cash method may be used by the following entities

   1.) Individuals

   2.) Partnerships that do not have C corporations as partners

   3.) Corporations or partnerships, if annual gross receipts for all prior years do not exceed $5 million

   4.) Certain farming businesses

   5.) Qualified personal service corporations in the fields of accounting, law, engineering, health, consulting, architecture, actuarial science, or performing arts

e. Exceptions for cash-basis taxpayers

   1.) Constructive receipt—if income is available, it is subject to income tax even though it is not physically in the taxpayer's possession

      a.) An example of this is accrued interest on a savings account. The interest is taxed to the depositor in the year it is available rather than in the year it is actually withdrawn.

   2.) Series E and Series EE bonds—the income on these savings bonds can be tax deferred

      a.) A cash-basis taxpayer has the choice to either (1) defer income recognition until maturity or redemption or (2) elect to include in gross income the annual increment in redemption value

         - Election to report the income from the bonds on an annual basis applies to all such bonds the taxpayer owns at the time of the election

   3.) Original issue discount (OID)

      a.) For OID, the Code treats cash-basis and accrual-basis taxpayers the same by requiring that the OID be reported when earned, regardless of the accounting method

EXAMPLE Peggy, a cash-basis taxpayer, has the following items of income for the current year:

- Salary of $40,000
- $5,000 bonus check issued and available at payroll office (but not picked up until January of the next year)
- Borrowed $10,000 on a home equity line of credit
- Original issue discount (OID) corporate bond, accrual amount of $2,000
- A US savings bond that increased in redemption value by $200. Last year, she elected to include the annual increment in redemption value in income.

Her gross income for the year is:

Salary	$40,000	
Bonus	5,000	(included because of constructive receipt rule)
OID	2,000	(although not received in cash, this is an exception for cash-basis taxpayers)
Savings bond	200	(she must be consistent in her election on this bond)
Total gross income	$47,200	

The proceeds from the home equity line of credit are not included in gross income because Peggy is obligated to repay.

2. Accrual method
   a. Requires reporting of expenses when incurred and income when earned for any single tax year
   b. Expenses do not have to be paid to be deductible, nor does income have to be received to be taxable
      1.) The controlling factor is when the income was earned or the expenses were incurred
   c. Exceptions for accrual-basis taxpayers
      1.) Prepaid income—for tax purposes, prepaid income is taxed in the year of receipt. Prepaid rents and prepaid interest may not be deferred by the accrual-basis taxpayer.
      2.) Deferral of advance payments for goods—a taxpayer can elect to defer recognition of income for advance payments for goods if the method of accounting for the sale is the same for tax and financial reporting
      3.) Deferral of advance payments for services—taxpayers can defer recognition of income for advance payments for services to be performed by the end of the tax year following the year of receipt
         a.) If the taxpayer might be required to perform any services after the tax year following the year of receipt of the advance payment, then the recognition must be no later than the year following the tax year of receipt

> **EXAMPLE** Julia, an accrual-basis taxpayer, owns an office building. On December 1 of the current year she rented the unit to a tenant who had a rather poor credit history. As a result, she asked him for a year's rent in advance, which amounted to $18,000. Julia must include the entire $18,000 rent in gross income in the current year.

3. Inventory methods

   a. Two commonly used methods to establish the cost of business inventory

      1.) First in, first out (FIFO)—inventory with the earliest purchase date is expensed to cost of goods sold first (first-in, first-out)

         a.) For example, if a business uses the FIFO method in an environment of rising prices, the cost of goods sold will be lower, and the amount of business taxable income will be higher

      2.) Last in, first out (LIFO)—the last inventory purchased is expensed to cost of goods sold (last-in, first-out)

         a.) If LIFO is used, the cost of goods sold will be higher, and the amount of business taxable income will be lower

      3.) The choice of inventory method a business makes has a significant impact on the amount of taxable income that is reported

   b. Converting from FIFO to LIFO (or vice versa) will also impact the amount of earnings reported to shareholders; accordingly, companies will issue earnings notices to the market whenever a change in inventory costing method is imminent

   c. FIFO/LIFO methods are also used when accounting for taxable earnings in some investments

      1.) If FIFO is used/required, then withdrawals from an investment will consist of basis to the extent of the taxpayer's basis in the investment, and then taxable earnings on the investment on the amount that is in excess of the nontaxable return of basis

      2.) If LIFO is used/required, then withdrawals from an investment will be considered taxable earnings to the extent of the earnings in the investment, and any excess over earnings will be nontaxable return of basis

      3.) The tax code will determine which method is used for the different types of investments

4. Long-term contracts

   a. In general

      1.) Any contract for the manufacture, building, installation, or construction of property

      2.) The contract must not be completed within the same year into which it was entered

      3.) A manufacturing contract must involve the manufacture of a unique item not normally carried in inventory (such as machinery) and normally requires more than 12 months to manufacture

4.) Must be accounted for using the percentage-of-completion method

a.) Home construction contracts and contracts of small businesses can be accounted for using the completed contract method

b. Percentage-of-completion method

1.) Requires the taxpayer to recognize a portion of the gross profit on the contract as based on the estimated percentage of the contract completed

2.) The portion of the contract price reportable in a given year is based on the following ratio:

$$\text{Total contract price} \times \left(\frac{\text{costs incurred during the current period}}{\text{total estimated costs for the contract}} \right)$$

3.) More accurately matches income and expenses of the project to taxable income

EXAMPLE In Year 1, Johnson Corporation entered into a contract to build a hotel that will be completed by December Year 2. The contract price was $2 million, and the estimated cost of construction was $1 million. During Year 1, actual costs incurred were $600,000. In Year 2, the hotel was completed at a total cost of $1,100,000. Johnson Corporation will report the following income in Year 1 and Year 2:

	Year 1	Year 2
Revenue reported on tax return	$1,200,000*	$800,000
(Costs)	(600,000)	(500,000)
Net income	$600,000	$300,000

*($600,000 ÷ $1,000,000) = 60% × $2,000,000 = $1,200,000

4.) If less than 10% of the total estimated contract costs have been incurred, may defer reporting the revenue until the year in which the 10% threshold has been reached

5.) Special look-back provisions apply in the tax year the contract is completed

a.) Annual income must be recalculated on the basis of actual final costs rather than on estimated costs

b.) Interest will be owed by or payable to the taxpayer if there was an underpayment or overpayment for any tax year

EXAMPLE Assuming the same facts as in the previous example, Johnson Corporation's net income should have been $490,000 in Year 1, as calculated below. Johnson overstated income by $110,000 (reported $600,000 less $490,000). As a result, the IRS is required to pay Johnson interest on the overpayment of the related tax.

	Year 1
Revenue based on actual costs	$1,090,000
(Costs)	(600,000)
Net income	$490,000

*($600,000 ÷ $1,100,000) = 54.5% × $2,000,000 = $1,090,000

Year 2 income would also be adjusted for the difference.

	Year 2
Revenue based on actual costs	$910,000
(Costs)	(500,000)
Net income	$410,000

*This figure does not include any interest income from the IRS, which is not part of the calculation.

c. Completed contract method

1.) Allows the taxpayer to defer revenue recognition until the contract is completed

2.) Can only be used in two situations

a.) Home construction contracts—at least 80% of the costs are related to buildings containing no more than four dwelling units

b.) Small contractors—contracts completed within two years by contractors with average annual gross receipts (for the last three years) of $10 million or less

d. Alternative minimum tax (AMT) consequences

1.) The percentage-of-completion method must be used for AMT purposes, except for home construction contracts, which can use the completed contract method

2.) If a small contractor uses the completed contract method for regular tax purposes, there will be an AMT adjustment required each year of the contract

3.) There is no AMT adjustment required for home construction contracts

5. Installment sales

a. See XVIII. Property Transactions—Topic L—Installment Sales for details on the installment method of accounting

6. Hybrid method
   a. A combination of the accrual and cash methods of accounting
   b. The taxpayer may account for some items of income using the accrual method (e.g., sales) and other items using the cash method (e.g., interest income)
7. Accounting method changes
   a. Once an accounting method has been adopted, it can only be changed with approval from the IRS
   b. Changes in accounting methods may include the following
      1.) A change from the cash to accrual basis
      2.) A change in inventory valuation [e.g., first in, first out (FIFO) to last in, first out (LIFO)]
      3.) A change from the completed contract method to the percentage-of-completion method for long-term contracts
   c. Taxpayers who change their method of accounting must make certain adjustments to income in the year of the change (or over a longer period if certain conditions are met)
      1.) The adjustments are necessary to prevent the omission or duplication of income and deductions

> **EXAMPLE** Katrina Enterprises is a corporation that switched from the cash method of accounting to the accrual method of accounting this year. At the end of last year, the company's outstanding receivables were $40,000. If Katrina Enterprises were allowed to switch to the accrual method of accounting without an income adjustment, $40,000 would completely escape taxation. The company must report $40,000 of income this year as a result of the change in accounting method.

   d. Correction of an error on a tax return
      1.) An error, such as a mathematical mistake, can be corrected on an amended return without IRS approval
      2.) If the correction changes the amount of tax due, interest and penalties may apply or a refund may be due to the taxpayer

D. INCOME SOURCES

1. Tax law doctrines have been developed by the IRS and courts to guide practitioners in regard to what is proper (versus abusive) tax management. The following doctrines are the most accepted of these administratively imposed theories.
   a. Business purpose doctrine—This doctrine stipulates that a transaction will not be effective for income tax purposes unless it is intended to achieve a genuine business purpose other than tax avoidance. An example is a high-tax-bracket, individual taxpayer forming a regular corporation simply to take advantage of the lower rates afforded to the corporation on the sale or disposition of assets. In this case, the corporate entity will be ignored because it lacks a valid business purpose.

b. Substance-over-form doctrine—This doctrine allows the IRS to look through the legal formalities of a transaction to determine its actual economic substance. If the substance differs from the form, the IRS will determine the tax consequences of the transaction on the basis of its reality rather than its illusion. An example is a corporate executive who has her corporation lend her needed money rather than receive it as income. In this case, the IRS will likely tax the loan proceeds as in lieu of salary.

c. Step-transaction doctrine—The step-transaction doctrine allows the IRS to collapse a series of apparently unrelated transactions into only one transaction to determine the tax consequences. An example is the sale of property by a corporation to an unrelated purchaser who subsequently resells the property to a wholly named subsidiary of the corporation. The IRS will likely collapse the two transactions into a direct sale of property from the corporation to its subsidiary and apply the appropriate specific tax rules.

d. Assignment-of-income doctrine—This doctrine is generally well-known under the colloquial term *the fruit and the tree*. According to a famous US Supreme Court case, a taxpayer who earns income and is the source of that income (i.e., the tree) cannot assign that income (i.e., the fruit) to someone else for income tax purposes (i.e., separate the fruit from the tree). As a result, the taxpayer will be taxed on that income.

EXAMPLE Jill, who is in the highest income tax bracket, directs her employer to pay $18,000 of her salary to her son, who is a college student in the lowest income tax bracket. Jill cannot assign the income to her son. If her employer pays the money to her son, her W-2 will include the $18,000, and she will have been deemed to have made a gift to her son of $18,000. She will be required to file a gift tax return.

e. Tax benefit rule or doctrine—This rule converts otherwise nontaxable receipts into taxable income. The most common example is when a taxpayer is reimbursed in a subsequent year for medical expenses paid and deducted in a previous year. Because the taxpayer has received a tax benefit via the previous year's medical deduction, the application of the rule results in the taxability of subsequent medical reimbursements (an otherwise nontaxable item).

1.) For example, a taxpayer who claims the standard deduction in Year 1 receives a $500 state income tax refund in Year 2. The refund is not taxable because the taxpayer did not deduct the state income taxes paid. If the taxpayer had claimed $12,000 of itemized deductions in Year 1, the $500 refund would have been taxable in Year 2.

f. Constructive receipt doctrine or rule—If there is no substantial limitation or restriction on a taxpayer's right to bring the funds under personal control, the income is taxed to a taxpayer as though it had actually been received

1.) For example, a payroll check issued December 31 by an employer and available to be picked up by the employee on that date is income for that year. Delaying the check retrieval from the employer until January of the next year does not change the fact that the taxpayer had the right to it (constructive receipt) in the prior year.

2.) Common examples of constructive receipt include matured and payable bond interest coupons, interest credited on savings bank deposits, and dividends on stock made payable at the shareholder's demand or personal request

2. Personal services

   a. When an employee renders services to the employer's customer, the employer is taxed on the income received from the customer

      1.) The employer pays deductible compensation to the employee who receives taxable compensation

3. Income from property—income from property, such as stocks, bonds, and rental property, must be included in the gross income of the owner of the property

   a. Interest is accrued daily

   b. Dividends are paid at the discretion of the corporation and, unlike interest, do not accrue daily

      1.) Paid from corporate earnings and profits

      2.) Accrue after declaration and date of record

      3.) Dividends are taxed to the person who is entitled to receive them

      4.) If a taxpayer sells stock after a dividend has been declared but before the record date, the dividend will be taxed to the purchaser instead of the seller (determined by date of record)

      5.) Dividends may be paid in cash or property

   c. Phantom income

      1.) Taxable income that has not yet been received in cash

      2.) Investor's basis is increased each year by the amount of interest income recognized

   d. The income-producing property must also be assigned for the income to be taxed to the assignee.

EXAMPLE

- Joe, a taxpayer in the highest income tax bracket, owns rental property that generates $2,000 of rental income per month. Joe instructs the tenant of his rental property to pay the rent to Joe's daughter, Mary, who is in the 15% income tax bracket. Because Joe owns the rental property, the payment of rent to his daughter will be an assignment of income. Joe will be taxed on the rental income, even though his daughter received the actual payments.
- Cornelius owns 20 shares of Qualco stock. Qualco declares a dividend on September 1 for shareholders of record September 15, payable October 15. If Cornelius sells his shares on September 16, he still will have dividend income, even though he did not own the stock at the dividend payment date, because he held it on the date of record.

4. Income from partnerships, S corporations, trusts, and estates
    a. Partnerships and S corporations are pass-through entities
        1.) Partnerships
            a.) Income from partnerships is taxed to the partners at their own individual rates
            b.) The partnership must file an informational return (Form 1065)
            c.) Each partner receives a K-1 indicating his share of the partnership income
            d.) Income from a general partnership on the K-1 is typically self-employment income
        2.) S corporations
            a.) The shareholders, rather than the corporation, pay the tax on an S corporation's income
            b.) An S corporation files Form 1120S
            c.) Each shareholder receives a K-1 indicating his share of the S corporation's income
            d.) A shareholder who is also an employee of the S corporation will receive a W-2 for the earned income (wages)
    b. Income in respect of a decedent (IRD)—income generated by assets of an estate that is distributed from the estate to the beneficiaries is generally taxable
    c. Income generated by assets of a trust that is distributed from the trust to the beneficiaries is generally taxable
        1.) Any income not distributed is generally taxed to the estate or trust, according to the estate and trust tax schedule

> **EXAMPLE** Carla is a calendar-year taxpayer. She receives a K-1 on March 1 of the current year, from a partnership that has a January 31 year-end. The income will be included on her current year tax return because she must report her partnership distributive share for the partnership tax year ending in her tax year.

5. Income in community property states
    a. One-half of the earnings of each spouse during marriage is considered to be owned by the other spouse (a one-half undivided individual interest)
    b. Community property for spouses living apart—a spouse (or former spouse) will be taxed only on their own actual earnings from personal services if all of the following conditions are met
        1.) The spouses live apart for the entire year
        2.) They do not file a joint return
        3.) No portion of the earned income was transferred between the spouses

6. Conduit for others
   a. The taxpayer obtains possession of the income but is not legally entitled to the receipt of the income because the taxpayer is required to turn over the income to its rightful owner
   b. For example, a professor conducts a seminar for the public, but because he does it as the employee of the university, he must turn over the student fees to the university because he is only a conduit for the fees. The income is not his own.

E. ALIMONY AND SEPARATE MAINTENANCE PAYMENTS

1. Alimony and separate maintenance payments are deductible by the payor and are includable in the gross income of the payee
2. Post-1984 divorce agreements and decrees
   a. Payments are classified as alimony only if all of the following conditions are satisfied:
      1.) The payments are made in cash (although if the payee spouse owns life insurance on the life of the payor, the premium payments made by the payor for that spouse will qualify as cash for this purpose)
      2.) The agreement or decree does not specify that the payments are not alimony for federal income tax purposes
      3.) The payee and payor are not members of the same household at the time the payments are made
      4.) There is no liability to make the payments for any period after the death of the payee
      5.) Payments are made directly to payee spouse or to a third party for direct benefit of payee spouse (e.g., making the mortgage payment, health insurance premiums for ex-spouse and/or children)
3. Front-loading (also referred to as alimony recapture)
   a. A measure to discourage disguising property settlements as alimony
   b. If there is more than a $15,000 decrease in alimony payments between any of the first three years, there may be alimony recapture
   c. The formula to calculate alimony recapture

$$R_3 = R_1 + R_2$$

$$R_2 = P_2 - (P_3 + 15{,}000)$$

$$R_1 = P_1 - \left[\frac{(P_2 - R_2 + P_3)}{2} + \$15{,}000\right]$$

R_1 = Recapture Year 1 — P_1 = Payments Year 1

R_2 = Recapture Year 2 — P_2 = Payments Year 2

R_3 = Recapture Year 3 — P_3 = Payments Year 3

NOTE: R_2 cannot be less than zero. If you get a negative number, set R_2 equal to zero.

d. A shortcut in calculating recapture for Year 3 is $R_3 = P_1 + P_2 - 2P_3 - \$37,500$

e. Alimony recapture affects the third year of alimony payments only

1.) R_3 will be claimed as income by the original payor and claimed as a deduction from income by the payee

2.) The effect of the original transaction is reversed. (No cash changes hands; this is merely a tax transaction.)

f. Divorcing taxpayers may purposely create alimony recapture where the payor's income tax bracket in the third year is expected to be less than the bracket in the first year and where the payee's bracket in the third year is expected to be greater than in the first year

1.) Requires the divorcing parties to agree on the strategy

> **EXAMPLE** Dave and Sue's divorce became final on January 2 of the current year. Dave is an executive for a Fortune 500 company, and Sue is starting her own business this year. In the current year (year 1 of the divorce agreement), Dave expects his marginal income tax rate to be 35% and Sue's marginal income tax rate will be 25% because of some start-up expenses of her new business. Two years from now (year 3 of the divorce agreement), Dave will retire and will be in the 15% tax bracket and Sue's business, a sole proprietorship, will cause her to be in the 35% tax bracket. Dave intentionally front-loaded his alimony payments to Sue ($60,000 in year 1, $40,000 in year 2, and $20,000 in year 3), resulting in alimony recapture for Dave of $22,500 (see previous example for calculation of recapture amount) in year 3.
>
> In year 1, Dave will get a deduction of $60,000, when his tax rate is 35%. Sue will include the alimony received in her gross income, when her tax rate is only 25%.
>
> In year 3, Dave must report (in his gross income) the alimony recapture of $22,500, when his tax rate will be only 15%. Sue will receive a deduction of $22,500, when her tax rate is 35%.

g. Property transfers between divorcing spouses

1.) Must occur within one year after marriage ceases or is related to the divorce

2.) No gain or loss recognized by transferor

3.) No deduction received for transferor

4.) Not included in gross income of transferee

5.) Basis to transferee spouse-former spouse is same as transferor spouse's basis immediately before transfer

6.) If transferee spouse-former spouse is nonresident alien, transferor must recognize gain or loss

7.) If liabilities assumed by recipient spouse-former spouse exceed transferor's basis, non-recognition is unavailable, and the transferee spouse's basis in the property is increased by the amount of any gain recognized

F. CHILD SUPPORT

1. Money received for child support is not includable as taxable income by the payee and is not deductible by the payor
   a. If payments to a former spouse are reduced when the child reaches a certain age, marries, or dies, the amount of the reduction is presumed to be child support and the remainder is considered alimony if it meets the alimony criteria
   b. For example, if one parent is required to pay life insurance premiums on a policy of a child, the premiums are not deductible by the payor as alimony because the premium is considered child support for that child

> **EXAMPLE** As part of their divorce agreement, David must pay Michelle $4,000 per month. In five years, when their daughter attains age 18, the payments are reduced to $2,800 per month.
>
> The reduction of $1,200 ($4,000 – $2,800) will be considered child support and will never be deductible by David.

G. INTEREST ON BELOW-MARKET LOANS

1. Where a lender has issued a below-market-rate loan, the lender may be required to impute (recognize) interest income or the borrower may receive an interest expense deduction when, in fact, no interest has been received or paid
   a. Imputed interest is calculated using the federal government's borrowing rate, compounded semiannually and adjusted monthly
   b. If the interest charged on the loan is less than the federal rate, the imputed interest is the difference in interest determined using the federal rate and the interest determined using the actual rate
2. The imputed interest rules apply to the following types of below-market-rate loans
   a. Gift loans—the lender has interest income and the borrower has interest expense to the extent of imputed interest. In addition, a gift has been made to the borrower in the amount of imputed interest.
   b. Compensation-related loans—employer loans to employees. The corporation has interest income and compensation expense for the amount of the imputed interest. The borrower will have compensation income and interest expense, which may or may not be deductible, in the same amount.
   c. Corporation-shareholder loans—a loan to a nonemployee shareholder by the corporation. The corporation will have interest income and a dividend distribution for the amount of the imputed interest. The shareholder-borrower will have dividend income and interest expense (may or may not be deductible) for the same amount.
   d. Tax avoidance loans—loans that significantly affect the borrower or lender's federal tax liability

3. Exceptions and limitations to the imputed interest rules

   a. No interest is imputed on total outstanding gift loans in the aggregate of $10,000 or less between individuals, unless the proceeds are used to purchase income-producing property

      1.) Also an exception for compensation-related or corporation-shareholder loans that are less than or equal to $10,000

   b. On loans between individuals greater than $10,000 and less than or equal to $100,000, the imputed interest cannot exceed the borrower's net investment income (from all sources) for the year

      1.) A further exception carved out by law states that if the borrower's net investment income for the year does not exceed $1,000, no interest is imputed on loans of $100,000 or less

   c. If the principal purpose of the loan is tax avoidance, none of the exceptions apply

> **EXAMPLE** On January 1, Richie loaned his daughter, Beth, $90,000 to purchase a new personal residence. There were no other loans outstanding between Richie and Beth. Beth's only income was $30,000 salary and $4,000 interest income. Richie had investment income of $200,000. Richie did not charge Beth interest. The relevant federal rate was 9%.
>
> Richie must recognize imputed interest income of $4,000. The $100,000 exemption applies, and thus Richie's imputed interest income (and Beth's imputed interest expense) is limited to Beth's net investment income. In addition, Richie is deemed to have made a gift to Beth of $4,000. The gift is eligible for the annual exclusion.

H. PRIZES AND AWARDS

1. Cash and the fair market value of prizes and awards are included in gross income
2. When the winner has an option of taking a lump sum or an annuity, if the annuity is chosen, the annuity payment is included in income each year

   a. If the winner chooses the option of a lump sum or an annuity payable over at least 10 years, the payment of winnings is considered made when actually paid

3. If the winner receives the award for religious, charitable, scientific, educational, artistic, literary, or civic achievement and turns the proceeds over to a governmental unit or qualifying charity, the award may be excluded from income

I. INCOME FROM ANNUITIES

1. As the value of the annuity increases, the owner or annuitant does not report any income because it has not been constructively received
2. Tax treatment of withdrawals before the scheduled annuity starting date

   a. Withdrawals (including loans) on contracts issued after August 13, 1982, are included in gross income up to total earnings (LIFO basis recovery)

      1.) Amounts received in excess of post-August 13, 1982—increases in cash value are treated as a recovery of capital until the taxpayer's cost has been entirely recovered

2.) The taxpayer may also be subject to a 10% penalty for early withdrawals unless he has attained age 59½, is deceased, or is disabled. This penalty will apply only to the taxable portion of the withdrawal.

b. Collections before the annuity start date on contracts issued on August 13, 1982, or earlier are subject to FIFO tax treatment so that adjusted tax basis is received first and is not taxable

3. Tax treatment of annuity payments received on and after the annuity starting date

a. The annuitant can exclude from taxation the portion of each payment that represents the return of investment basis (cost). The exclusion amount is calculated as follows:

$$\frac{\text{Investment basis}}{\text{Expected return}} \times \text{annuity payment} = \text{exclusion amount}$$

b. To determine the taxable amount, subtract the exclusion amount from the total annuity payment received. For retirement plan distributions, the IRS provides a simplified method for calculating exclusions.

c. For contracts issued on December 31, 1986, or earlier, the exclusion ratio is used for all payments, even if payments are made past the expected life expectancy. This allows the taxpayer to exclude more than his basis if he lives past life expectancy.

d. For contracts issued after December 31, 1986, the exclusion ratio is only used until all basis has been recovered. Thus, the taxpayer will not use the exclusion ratio for payments made after life expectancy and will be taxed on the entire amount received.

EXAMPLE Wendy, a 55-year-old taxpayer, has begun receiving an annuity over her life expectancy of 25.5 years. She receives $1,500 per month. Her contributions to the annuity were after tax and amounted to $91,800 (her basis). Payments began April 1 of this year. Wendy can exclude $2,700 of the annuity payments received this year.

Exclusion ratio is $91,800 ÷ $459,000* = 20%

20% × $1,500 × 9 months = $2,700

* $1,500 x 12 x 25.5

J. GROUP TERM LIFE INSURANCE

1. Employees can exclude premiums paid by their employers on the first $50,000 of group term life insurance

2. Only employees are eligible for the $50,000 exclusion (partners, proprietors, and greater than 2% S corporation owners are not employees)

3. If the group term life insurance amount exceeds $50,000, the taxable amount of the benefit is calculated by applying the premium from the Uniform Premium Table to the excess coverage [see Cost per $1,000 of Protection for One Month (Section 79)]

4. If the plan is discriminatory, key employees and highly-compensated employees lose the $50,000 exclusion

a. Must include in income the greater of the actual cost of the insurance or the premium calculated using the Uniform Premium Table

EXHIBIT 8: Cost per $1,000 of Protection for One Month (Section 79)

Age	Cost
Under 25	$ .05
25–29	$ .06
30–34	$ .08
35–39	$ .09
40–44	$ .10
45–49	$ .15
50–54	$ .23
55–59	$ .43
60–64	$ .66
65–69	$1.27
70 or older	$2.06

See Reg. 1.79-3(d)(2)

EXAMPLE Tom is 51 years old and works for Employer A. Tom's coverage with Employer A is $80,000. Tom pays premiums of $50 a year under the Employer A group plan.

Calculate the amount to include in Tom's income as follows:

Employer A coverage (in thousands)	$80
Less exclusion (in thousands)	($50)
Excess amount (in thousands)	$30
Multiply by cost per $1,000 per month, age 51 (from table)	× $.23
Cost of excess insurance for 1 month (.23 × 30)	$6.90
Multiply by number of full months' coverage at this cost	× 12
Cost of excess insurance for tax year	$82.80
Less premiums paid	($50.00)
Cost to include in income as wages (W-2)	$32.80

K. UNEMPLOYMENT COMPENSATION

1. Unemployment compensation benefits are included in gross income (in lieu of wages)

L. SOCIAL SECURITY BENEFITS

1. As much as 85% of Social Security benefits may be included in gross income
2. The amount subject to tax is based on the taxpayer's modified adjusted gross income
3. The taxable amounts can be determined by one of two formulas using the modified adjusted gross income (MAGI)
4. MAGI—AGI from all sources (less Social Security) plus the foreign income exclusion and any tax-exempt interest income
5. Calculation of the taxable amount
    a. Two base amounts are established
        1.) First base amount
            a.) $32,000 for married filing jointly
            b.) $0 for married taxpayers who do not live apart for the entire year but file a separate return
            c.) $25,000 for all other taxpayers
        2.) Second base amount
            a.) $44,000 for married individuals filing jointly
            b.) $0 for married taxpayers who do not live apart for the entire year but file a separate return
            c.) $34,000 for all other taxpayers
    b. Fifty percent of the excess over the first threshold plus 35% of the excess over the second threshold is included in AGI
        1.) The amount calculated above cannot exceed the lesser of:
            a.) 85% of the Social Security benefit, or
            b.) 50% of the Social Security benefit plus 85% of the excess over the second threshold.

M. FEDERAL INSURANCE CONTRIBUTIONS ACT (FICA) TAX

1. Consists of the Social Security tax (OASDI) and the Medicare tax (HI)
2. For OASDI, a tax rate of 6.2% is applied to wages, with a base cap of $106,800 in 2011 (indexed to changes in average wages)
    a. Employers must match this rate for employees
    b. Self-employed individuals pay a total OASDI rate of 12.4% on net income
3. The Medicare tax has no ceiling for earnings
    a. The HI tax is 1.45% for both the employee and the employer
    b. Self-employed taxpayers pay 2.9% on net income

4. Total self-employment taxes are 15.3%
    a. When calculating self-employment tax, the taxpayer reduces net earnings from self-employment by 50% of the self-employment rate
    b. In addition, the self-employed taxpayer may deduct one-half of the self-employment tax paid as a deduction for AGI
        1.) See Section VI (B) One-Half of Self-Employment Tax Paid for an example of the calculation

Planning Tips

- Because S corporation earnings (other than salaries) are not considered self-employment income, they are not subject to FICA tax and it may be possible, in some cases, to decrease salaries to avoid a portion of the FICA tax. However, the salaries paid must be reasonable.
- Structure payments to reflect rental or interest income that is not subject to FICA. Note, however, that rental of personal property may be subject to FICA.
- A shareholder in a personal service S corporation may want to accumulate funds in the S corporation, instead of personally, to avoid the FICA tax.

N. DEATH BENEFIT ONLY (DBO)

1. Amounts paid by an employer, upon an employee's death, to the employee's beneficiary(ies) are fully includable in the beneficiary's(ies') income
    a. These amounts are not a life insurance policy death benefit to the family; they are a cash fringe benefit paid by the employer upon the employee's death (and therefore are taxable)

V. GROSS INCOME—EXCLUSIONS

A. INTRODUCTION

1. Only items that are specifically excluded by statute are excludable from income
2. Generally, items excluded are donative in nature, a return of capital, socially desirable, or a matter of legislative grace, usually resulting from the lobbying efforts of a special interest group

EXHIBIT 9: Exclusions from Gross Income

Items Characterized by Love, Affection, or Assistance
Gifts, bequests, and inheritances (Section 102)
Scholarships for tuition and books (Section 117)
Life insurance proceeds paid by reason of death (Section 101)
Accelerated death benefits, including gain on sale of policy to a viatical settlement provider (Section 101)

Personal and Welfare Items
Injury or sickness payments (Section 104)
Amounts received under insurance contracts for certain living expenses (Section 123)
Reimbursement for the costs of caring for a foster child (Section 131)

Employer-Provided Benefits

- Fringe Benefits
  - Accident and health benefits (sections 105 and 106)
  - Medical/health savings accounts reimbursements (Section 106)
  - Long-term care insurance benefits (Section 7702)
  - Lodging and meals furnished for the convenience of the employer (Section 119)
  - Employee achievement awards (Section 74(c))
  - Employer contributions to employee group term life insurance (Section 79) (up to $50,000 coverage)
  - Benefits received through cafeteria plans (Section 125) (within limits)
  - Educational assistance payments (Section 127) (within limits)
  - Child or dependent care (within limits)
  - Services provided to employees at no additional cost to the employer (Section 132)
  - Employee discounts (Section 132)
  - Working condition and de minimis fringes (Section 132)
  - Athletic facilities provided to employees (Section 132)
  - Qualified transportation fringe benefit (Section 132)
  - Tuition reductions granted to employees of educational institutions (Section 117)
  - Adoption assistance (Section 137)
- Military Benefits
  - Combat pay (Section 112)
  - Housing, uniforms, and other benefits (Section 134)
- Foreign Earned Income
  - Choice between foreign earned income exclusion and foreign income credit (Section 911)

Investments
Interest on state and local government obligations (Section 103)
Gain exclusion (50%) for small business stock (Section 1202) (75% for stock acquired after 2/17/09 and before 9/27/10, and 100% of the gain is excluded for both regular tax and AMT for QSBS acquired after 9/27/10 and before 1/1/11)

Benefits for the Elderly

Social Security benefits (partial, see Gross Income—Inclusions Social Security Benefits) (Section 86)

Other Benefits
Income from discharge of indebtedness under bankruptcy or insolvency (Section 108)
Recovery of a prior year's deduction that yielded no tax benefit (Section 111)
Educational savings bonds (Section 135)
Gain from sale of personal residence—$250,000 single exclusion; $500,000 for married filing jointly (Section 121)

B. GIFTS, BEQUESTS, AND INHERITANCES

1. A gift is defined by the courts as a voluntary transfer of property by one to another without adequate (valuable) consideration
2. The recipient (donee) of a gift or inheritance is allowed to exclude the value of the property from gross income
   a. Inherited property deemed as income in respect of a decedent (IRD) is includable in the recipient's income
      1.) Character of the IRD is same for recipient as the decedent
      2.) An itemized income tax deduction not subject to the 2% of AGI floor will be allowed for the portion of estate tax attributable to the IRD (See *Volume 6—Estate Planning*)
   b. Income subsequently earned from the gift of income-producing property is subject to tax

C. SCHOLARSHIPS

1. Recipients must be a candidate for a degree
   a. May exclude from gross income amounts used for tuition and related expenses (books and fees but not room and board), provided the conditions of the grant do not require that the funds be used for other purposes
2. If the scholarship is received in one year and spent in the subsequent year, the student does not have to include in income the amount in excess of qualified expenses until all expenditures have been made
   a. Included in income in the year resolution occurs
3. Employees of nonprofit educational institutions are allowed to exclude a tuition waiver from gross income if the waiver is pursuant to a qualified tuition reduction plan
4. Payments by a donor made directly to an educational institution are qualified payments, are not includable in the student's income, and are not subject to gift tax

EXAMPLES

- On June 1, Year 1, Mark was awarded a full tuition scholarship for his freshman year at Old Elm University. He began his freshman year in August Year 1 and completed it in May Year 2. One half of the tuition is due August 1, Year 1, and one-half is due January 1, Year 2. Because the scholarship was for tuition only, nothing will be included in Mark's gross income in Year 1 or Year 2.
- On January 1, Year 1, David was awarded a postgraduate fellowship grant of $6,000 by a tax-exempt educational organization. David is not a candidate for a degree and was awarded the grant to continue his research. The grant was awarded for the period August 1, Year 1, through July 31, Year 2. On August 1, Year 1, David elected to receive the full amount of the grant. Because David is not a candidate for a degree, he must include all of the grant received on his Year 1 tax return. The issue of proration between years is not relevant in this example.

D. LIFE INSURANCE PROCEEDS

1. In general
   a. Proceeds paid to a beneficiary because of death of the insured are generally exempt from income tax
   b. If the proceeds are received in installment payments, any interest income will be taxable

> **EXAMPLE** Susan, a widow, elected to receive the proceeds of a $200,000 face value insurance policy on the life of her deceased husband in 10 annual installments of $22,000 each (beginning last year). In the current year, she received $22,000, which included $2,000 interest. Susan must include the $2,000 interest in her gross income.

   c. Dividends from a life insurance policy are not taxable income unless the aggregate dividends received exceed the taxpayer's basis in the contract
   d. Business use of life insurance
      1.) Taxpayers may not deduct life insurance premiums paid for insurance that covers the life of an officer, owner, or employee of the business if the taxpayer is directly or indirectly a beneficiary under the policy
2. Surrendering the policy before insured's death
   a. If the owner cancels the policy and receives the cash surrender value, the owner must recognize ordinary income gain to the extent the amount received exceeds the cost basis of the policy
      1.) Basis is generally the sum of premiums paid less dividends received
   b. Losses are not deductible
   c. Withdrawals or loans are received on a FIFO basis
      1.) Return of capital (basis) is nontaxable
3. Transfer-for-value rule
   a. If an existing policy is transferred for valuable consideration, the insurance proceeds are includable in the gross income of the transferee to the extent the proceeds exceed basis (amount paid for policy plus any subsequent premiums paid)
   b. Five instances in which the transfer-for-value will not result in inclusion in gross income
      1.) Transfers to the insured
      2.) Transfers to a partner of the insured
      3.) Transfers to a partnership in which the insured is a partner
      4.) Transfers to a corporation in which the insured is an officer or shareholder
      5.) Transfers to a transferee (such as a child), whose basis in the policy is determined by reference to the transferor's basis (tax-free exchange or gift)

4. Viatical and life settlements

   a. Amounts received under the sale of a life insurance contract on the life of a terminally ill or chronically ill individual are excluded from the recipient's gross income

      1.) Also applies to the sale/assignment of a contract to a qualified viatical settlement provider

   b. A terminally ill individual

      1.) Has been certified by a physician as having an illness or condition that can reasonably be expected to result in death within 24 months of the date of certification

   c. A chronically ill individual

      1.) Person who is unable to perform at least two activities of daily living (e.g., eating, bathing) for at least 90 days

      2.) Benefits will only be excluded from income to the extent they are used for long-term care services

   d. Under the transfer-for-value rule, the purchaser of the life insurance policy will be taxed on any benefits received in excess of the purchaser's basis

      1.) Purchaser's basis is the amount paid to the insured-owner plus subsequent premiums paid

> **EXAMPLE** Erwin was recently diagnosed with a rare liver disorder and was certified by his physician, on July 15 of the current year, as terminally ill. Erwin immediately resigned from his sales position with ABC Company and sold his life insurance policy with a face value of $500,000 to a viatical settlement provider (VSP) for $340,000. Erwin paid $30,000 in premiums over the last few years.
>
> Because Erwin was certified as terminally ill, none of the proceeds he received from the VSP will be taxable to him. If, instead, he were certified as chronically ill, the proceeds would be excluded from his gross income only to the extent the proceeds were used for long-term care services.

5. Revenue Ruling 2009-13—tax treatment for cash surrenders and sales of life insurance contracts when the sale was to a person unrelated to the insured and would suffer no economic loss upon the death of the insured

   a. Sale is not a viatical settlement

   b. Seller-insured is not terminally or chronically ill within the meaning of Section 101(g)(4)

   c. For both a term life insurance contract and a cash-value, whole life contract, the total of aggregate premiums paid on the contract must be determined, in addition to

      1.) Cash surrender value—the adjusted basis in the policy is determined by the aggregate premiums payment.

      2.) Amount taxed at ordinary income rates is the cash surrender value received less the adjusted basis

> **EXAMPLE** Jack surrendered to the insurer a whole life insurance policy with a cash value of $80,000 (there were no policy loans or distributions from the policy prior to the surrender). Jack had made $70,000 in aggregate payments on the policy. The cost of insurance was $11,000. The amount taxed at ordinary income rates is $10,000 ($80,000 – $70,000). The cost of insurance element does not affect the cash surrender.

d. Nonviatical sale of a life insurance policy by the seller-insured

1.) Sold to an unrelated person who will not suffer an economic loss at the death of the insured

2.) Part of the gain on the sale can receive capital gain treatment when it exceeds the cash surrender value of the policy

3.) Adjusted basis reduced by the cost of insurance element for the policy

4.) Buyer has basis in the life insurance policy that will be deducted from the death benefit received (transfer-for-value)

5.) Cost of insurance in a term policy is presumed to be the premium and the value is the unused premium

> **EXAMPLE** Jack instead sold the policy to Martin, who is both unrelated and will not suffer an economic loss at Jack's death, for $95,000. All other facts remain the same. The amount of gain in excess of the ordinary income component of the cash surrender value is capital gain. The total amount of gain is calculated as $95,000 – ($70,000 – 11,000), or $36,000. The ordinary income component of the total gain is calculated in the same manner as a cash surrender and is deducted from the total gain.
>
> To arrive at the amount taxed at long-term capital gain rates: $36,000 – ($80,000 – $70,000) = $26,000.
>
> If Jack had a term life insurance policy with a monthly premium of $600 and sold it to Martin, who is both unrelated and will not suffer an economic loss at Jack's death, for $25,000, the treatment is a little different. Jack has owned and paid the premiums of the term policy for 108 months, including the month of sale. Because the policy has no cash value, the cost-of-insurance in a term policy is presumed to be the premium. If Jack sold the policy to Martin on January 15, his basis would only be the remaining prepaid and unused premium of $300. Jack would have no ordinary income because there are no earnings in the policy, and the gain on the sale is all capital gain.
>
> Jack's basis in the policy is $300 (the remaining unused premium), and his capital gain is $24,700 ($25,000 – $300).

6. Modified endowment contract (MEC)

a. Life insurance policy issued after June 21, 1988, that fails the 7-pay test

1.) 7-pay test—contract is a MEC if the premiums paid during the first seven years of the contract exceed the total of the net level premiums that would have been paid if the policy provided for paid-up benefits after the seventh year

2.) Material change—an existing life insurance policy that undergoes a material change must pass the 7-pay test each time there is a material change to the policy; failure causes the policy to be considered a MEC

b. For withdrawals or loans from the MEC, basis is recovered last (LIFO)
   1.) Withdrawals (including loans) to the extent of earnings are currently taxed
   2.) MECs are also subject to a 10% penalty on the taxable part of any withdrawals or loans if they are made before the policyholder attains age 59½
c. Classification as a MEC does not affect the taxation of the death benefit
   1.) The death benefit is received by the beneficiary tax free, provided there has not been a transfer for value

E. COMPENSATION FOR INJURIES AND ILLNESS

1. Taxability of damages received
   a. Compensatory damages
      1.) If the damages are awarded for physical injury or sickness, the damages are excludable from gross income (special damages)
      2.) Personal, nonphysical damages (e.g., emotional distress, business reputation damages, breach of contract, age discrimination, sexual harassment, slander and libel, pain and suffering) must be included in gross income (general damages)
   b. Punitive damages received for a personal physical injury award are generally included in gross income
   c. Interest on damage awards for personal injury, both compensatory and punitive, is included in gross income
2. Workers' compensation amounts received are excluded by statute from gross income

F. EMPLOYER-PROVIDED BENEFITS

1. Accident and health plans
   a. Premiums—premiums paid by the employer for accident, health, and disability insurance policies are deductible by the employer and excludable from the employee's income
   b. Benefits paid under employer-sponsored health and accident plans
      1.) If the payments are received for the medical care of the employee, spouse, or dependents, the payments are not included in the taxpayer's income
      2.) Payments for permanent loss or the loss of the use of a member or function of the body or permanent disfigurement of the employee, spouse, or dependent are not included in the taxpayer's income
      3.) Other insurance benefits collected are included in gross income
      4.) If a taxpayer pays the cost of a disability policy with after-tax dollars, any subsequent benefits are not taxable
      5.) If the employer pays the premiums, the benefits are taxable

6.) If the employer and taxpayer each pay a portion of the premium, there will be a fractional allocation to the nontaxed benefits based on contributions to the plan

c. Employees are not taxed on the value of coverage under a long-term care plan provided by their employer. This exclusion does not apply if coverage is reimbursed under a tax-free flexible spending plan or provided through a cafeteria plan.

d. Contributions made by an employer to a medical savings plan or health savings account are not included in the employee's income

2. Meals and lodging

   a. Excludable by employee if furnished by the employer on the business premises for the employer's convenience

   b. If free lodging is an employee benefit, the employee must be required to accept it as a condition of employment to exclude it from income

> **EXAMPLE** Tom is the manager of a hotel. To be available in emergency situations, Tom's employer requires that he live in one of the hotel rooms without charge. The value of the room is $1,500 per month if occupied each night. The hotel is ordinarily 70% occupied. If Tom did not live there, he would live in an apartment that would rent for $900 per month. The room is furnished for the convenience of the employer on the employer's premises and is a requirement of Tom's employment. Tom will not be required to report the benefit as income.

3. Group term life insurance—see Group Term Life Insurance in Section IV(J)

4. Child and dependent care services—employees can exclude up to $5,000 in child care expenses paid by their employer to enable the employee to work

   a. Exclusion is limited to the income of the lesser-paid spouse for married taxpayers

   b. Child care provided under a cafeteria plan is not eligible for the dependent care credit

5. Athletic facility provided to employees—the value of a health facility or gymnasium provided by the employer on the premises solely for the use of employees and the employee's dependents is excluded from the employee's gross income

   a. Employer-paid health club dues (public health club) for an employee are taxable income to the employee

6. Educational assistance (at the time of printing, this benefit was not extended by Congress for 2011)

   a. Qualified employer-provided educational assistance is excluded from gross income

   b. The exclusion is subject to an annual ceiling of $5,250

   c. Applies to both undergraduate and graduate education

   d. Cannot discriminate in favor of highly compensated employees (HCEs)

7. Cafeteria plans (Section 125)

   a. Employer offers the employee the choice between cash or selected nontaxable benefits

   b. If the employee chooses the benefit, it remains nontaxable
   c. If the employee chooses cash equal to the cost of the benefit, the cash is included in income
   d. Can also give employees opportunity to buy certain benefits with after-tax contributions

8. No additional cost services—excluded from income under the following conditions
   a. The employee receives services, not property
   b. The employer does not incur substantial additional cost, including forgone revenue, in providing the services to the employee
   c. The services are offered to customers in the ordinary course of the business in which the employee works (e.g., travel privileges for employees of an airline)
   d. Nondiscrimination provision—if the plan is discriminatory in favor of highly compensated employees, the highly compensated are denied exclusion treatment
9. Qualified employee discounts—when an employer offers goods or services to an employee at a discount, the discount can be excluded from income in the following cases
   a. In the case of property, it is not real property or investment personal property
   b. The property or services are offered in the same line of business in which the employee works
   c. In the case of property, the exclusion is limited to the gross profit component of the price to customers
   d. In the case of services, the exclusion is limited to 20% of the customer price
   e. Nondiscrimination provision—if the plan is discriminatory in favor of highly compensated employees, the highly compensated are denied exclusion treatment
10. Working condition fringes—when an employer provides property or services to an employee that an employee could have deducted had he paid for them himself, the value of the property or services is a nontaxable fringe
    a. Discrimination does not affect the exclusion status

> **EXAMPLE** Frances is a member of her state CPA society. Her employer pays the annual dues. This is a nontaxable fringe because Frances could have deducted the dues as an employee business expense had she paid them herself.

11. De minimis fringes—the benefits are so small that accounting for them is impractical
    a. The value of de minimis fringes are excludable
    b. For example, the personal use of a company-owned computer or copy machine is considered a nontaxable de minimis fringe benefit
    c. Discrimination does not affect the exclusion status
    d. Occasional tickets to cultural or sporting events, but not season tickets

12. Qualified transportation fringes—to encourage mass transit for commuting to and from work, this fringe benefit is nontaxable and includes the following
    a. Transportation in a commuter highway vehicle between the employee's residence and the place of work
    b. A transit pass within limits ($120 per month for 2011)
    c. Qualified parking within limits ($230 per month for 2011)
    d. The dollar limits are adjusted annually for inflation
13. Employer-provided adoption assistance
    a. Employer benefit payments or reimbursements of adoption expenses may be excluded from the employee's gross income
    b. Each of the following requirements must be met to exclude the benefits
        1.) The employer has a written adoption assistance plan
        2.) The plan does not discriminate in favor of highly compensated employees or their dependents
        3.) 5% or less of total payments made each year by the plan go to shareholders owning more than 5% of the company's stock
        4.) Employees are given adequate notice of their eligibility to participate in the plan
        5.) Payments or reimbursements are traceable to qualified employee adoption expenses
    c. An employee may exclude only a limited amount of benefits from gross income for each adoption effort, as indexed for inflation each year ($13,360 in 2011)
    d. The adoption exclusion and the adoption credit may both be used for the same adoption as long as the combination doesn't exceed the limit amount, or produce a double benefit
    e. The adoption exclusion is phased out for taxpayers with modified adjusted gross income above indexed limits ($185,210–$225,210 in 2011)
14. Employer-provided auto—personal use of an employer-provided car is usually a taxable fringe benefit
    a. The taxable amount is determined by the employer and included on the employee's W-2
15. See Summary of Fringe Benefits for a summary of fringe benefit exclusions, along with the effect of discriminatory application

d. When a creditor forecloses on a piece of property, it is treated as a sale or exchange

e. In some special instances, the taxpayer is allowed to reduce the basis of the asset by the realized gain from discharge of debt. Included are discharge of qualified real property business indebtedness, a seller's cancellation of the buyer's indebtedness, and forgiveness of student loans.

f. Students who are granted loans that are forgiven in return for working in the state after graduation do not have to include the debt forgiveness in their income

g. The Mortgage Debt Relief Act of 2007 generally allows taxpayers to exclude income from the discharge of debt on their principal residence. This provision applies to debt forgiven in calendar years 2007 through 2012. Up to $2 million of forgiven debt is eligible for this exclusion ($1 million if married filing separately).

2. Foreign earned income

a. The United States taxes all income of its citizens regardless of where it is earned. Without special provisions, US taxpayers could be in danger of having non-US income taxed twice, once by the United States and again by the foreign country.

b. The following options are available to mitigate double taxation

1.) Include the foreign income in taxable income and then claim a credit for foreign taxes paid

2.) Exclude up to $92,900 (for 2011) of the foreign earnings from US gross income

c. Foreign earned income is the earnings from the taxpayer's personal services in a foreign country

d. To qualify for the exclusion, the taxpayer must be either

1.) a bona fide resident of the foreign country; or

2.) present in a foreign country for at least 330 days during any 12 consecutive months

e. The exclusion is limited to an indexed amount per year. A taxpayer who is present in the country for less than the entire year must prorate the exclusion using the following formula:

$$\text{Maximum exclusion} \times \left(\frac{\text{number of days present in foreign country}}{\text{number of days in entire year}}\right)$$

f. Taxpayers who live and work abroad may elect to exclude amounts for employer-provided foreign housing costs

I. EDUCATIONAL INCENTIVES

1. Coverdell Education Savings Accounts (as of time of printing, Congress has not prevented the implementation of pre-EGTRRA rules)

a. Contributions

1.) Up to $500 per beneficiary (under 18) may be contributed to a Coverdell Education Savings Account

2.) The contribution is phased out at certain modified adjusted gross income (MAGI) levels. MAGI is defined as AGI increased by any excluded foreign earned income.

a.) The $500 contribution is phased out at the following MAGI levels, which do not adjust for inflation

Taxpayer Filing Status	MAGI Phaseout
Single	$95,000–$110,000
Married filing jointly	$150,000–$160,000

3.) A taxpayer may contribute to both a Coverdell Savings Account and a qualified tuition plan (QTP) for the same beneficiary in the same year

b. Distributions and rollovers

1.) Distributions used to pay qualified education expenses of an eligible student are excluded from income

a.) Includes tuition, fees, books, supplies, equipment, and special needs services

b.) Room and board are also included if the student attends on at least a half-time basis

2.) The amounts must be distributed to the beneficiary by age 30 if not used. Then, the accumulated earnings are taxable and subject to a 10% penalty.

3.) May be rolled over, free of taxation and penalty, to the account of a new beneficiary who is a member of the same family

4.) A taxpayer may claim the Hope Scholarship Tax Credit or the Lifetime Learning Credit for a taxable year and also exclude from gross income amounts distributed from a Coverdell Education Savings Account on behalf of the same student, provided the distribution is not used for the same educational expenses for which a credit is claimed

5.) Eligible educational institutions are generally accredited postsecondary schools offering associate's, bachelor's, or graduate-level or professional degrees

a.) Proprietary and postsecondary vocational schools are generally eligible

b.) Public, private, or religious elementary and secondary schools are also eligible

2. Qualified higher education expenses—as of the time of printing of the material, Congress has allowed this deduction to expire December 31, 2009

3. Qualified tuition plans (Section 529 plans)

a. Earnings on qualified tuition plans accumulate tax free

b. Distributions from qualified tuition programs are excluded from gross income to the extent that the distribution is used to pay for qualified higher education expenses

c. A taxpayer can claim the Hope Scholarship Tax Credit or Lifetime Learning Credit for a taxable year and also exclude from gross income amounts distributed from a qualified tuition program on behalf of the same student (provided the distribution is not used for the same expenses for which a credit is claimed)

d. A transfer from one qualified tuition program for the benefit of a designated beneficiary to another qualified tuition program for the benefit of the same beneficiary (rollover) is not considered a distribution

e. May be rolled over, free of taxation and penalty, to the account of a new beneficiary who is a member of the same family

4. See Retirement Planning outline for a discussion of tax incentives available through traditional IRAs and Roth IRAs
5. See "Interest on Educational Loans" in Section VI(L)
6. See "Cafeteria Plans" in Section V(F)(7)
7. Teacher's classroom expense—as of the time of printing of the material, Congress has allowed this deduction to expire December 31, 2009

VI. DEDUCTIONS FOR ADJUSTED GROSS INCOME

These deductions are subtracted from a taxpayer's gross income to arrive at adjusted gross income. Deductions for adjusted gross income (AGI) are discussed in the following section.

A. ORDINARY AND NECESSARY EXPENSES INCURRED IN A TRADE OR BUSINESS

1. Expenses related to a taxpayer's trade or business are deductions for AGI
2. Reported on Schedule C of an individual's Form 1040 (with the gross revenue) if the individual is a sole proprietor
3. Farm income and expenses are reported on Schedule F of Form 1040
4. Unreimbursed business expenses of an employee are deductible as miscellaneous itemized deductions, subject to the 2% of AGI floor (a deduction **from** AGI)
   a. Includes professional dues, union dues, uniforms, trade and professional journals, job-related education, unreimbursed travel, and other job-related expenses

B. ONE-HALF OF SELF-EMPLOYMENT TAX PAID

1. Self-employed individuals are allowed a deduction for AGI of one-half of self-employment tax paid
2. Self-employment tax is based on net income from self-employment
3. If net earnings from self-employment are less than $400 in any one year, no self-employment tax is payable
4. The steps to calculate the self-employment tax for 2011 where net income from self-employment is at or below the taxable wage base are as follows
   a. Calculate self-employment income
   b. Multiply the net earnings from self-employment by .9235
   c. Multiply the resulting product by .153 (the full self-employment tax rate)
   d. For the deductible self-employment tax, divide the product by 2
   e. Or, net SE income × .9235 ×.153 = self-employment tax due on the self-employment income ÷ 2 = deductible self-employment tax
   f. Alternative formula: net SE income × .1413 (or .9235 × .153) = self-employment tax due ÷ 2 = deductible self-employment tax

> **EXAMPLE** Paul has net Schedule C income of $40,000. His self-employment tax due would be $5,652 ($40,000 × .9235 × .153 = $5,651.82). His self-employment tax deduction is one-half of this amount equalling $2,826 ($5.652 ÷ 2). Using the alternative formula: $40,000 × .1413 = $5,562 self-employment tax due ÷ 2 = $2,826 deductible self-employment tax.

b. Travel to the new location (including lodging) and out-of-pocket travel (subject to the IRS mileage limit; indexed annually)
   1.) No meal deduction is allowed
   2.) No house-hunting expenses are deductible
   3.) No temporary living expenses are deductible

c. Tax treatment
   1.) Qualified expenditures reimbursed/paid by the employer are not reported on the employee's Form W-2 (and employer payment is not included in income)
   2.) Qualified, unreimbursed expenditures are deductible by the taxpayer for AGI
   3.) Nonqualified expenditures paid by or reimbursed by the employer are included in the employee's gross income and deducted by the employer as compensation

G. FORFEITED INTEREST PENALTY FOR PREMATURE WITHDRAWAL OF TIME DEPOSITS

1. Any forfeited interest on withdrawals from certificates of deposit (CDs) is deductible for AGI

> **EXAMPLE** Dan has an immediate need for a large amount of cash, and his most liquid asset is a three-year CD that does not mature for 18 more months. When he redeems the CD early, the bank charges him three months' interest as a penalty. The three months' interest is reportable as income, but it is also a deduction for AGI.

H. CAPITAL LOSSES

1. Capital losses can offset capital gains without limit
   a. Capital losses are deductible against a taxpayer's ordinary income up to $3,000 annually, with an unlimited carryforward amount
   b. Any capital losses unused after filing a taxpayer's final federal income tax return are lost and may not be used by the estate or a beneficiary
   c. A corporation can use capital losses only as an offset against capital gains
      1.) Capital losses in excess of a year's capital gains may be carried forward for five years or carried back to each of the preceding three tax years
      2.) Treated as a short-term capital loss for the year in which it is carried forward or back
      3.) Remaining capital losses that cannot be fully utilized in the carry-over periods (three years back and five years forward) are not deductible
2. See Section XVIII for rules and limitations on capital losses

I. SELF-EMPLOYED HEALTH INSURANCE PREMIUMS

1. Self-employed taxpayers and wage earners who are more than 2% shareholders of an S corporation can take a 100% deduction (not to exceed net earnings from self-employment) for amounts paid for health insurance for taxpayers, spouses, and dependents

J. CONTRIBUTIONS TO ARCHER MEDICAL SAVINGS ACCOUNTS (ARCHER MSAs)

1. Employees of small employers (50 or fewer employees) and self-employed individuals with high-deductible health insurance plans can make tax-deductible contributions to an Archer MSA and use the funds accumulated in the Archer MSA to pay medical expenses. If the employer makes the contributions, they are excluded from the employee's income.
2. Earnings generated by the plan are not taxable, and distributions from an Archer MSA used to pay medical expenses are not taxable
3. Distributions not used for medical expenses are taxable and subject to a 20% penalty tax. The 20% penalty does not apply to distributions made after age 65 or upon death or disability.
4. No new Archer MSAs may be opened but existing accounts can be maintained

K. CONTRIBUTIONS TO HEALTH SAVINGS ACCOUNTS (HSAs)

1. HSAs have characteristics similar to the MSAs. A person can have both an MSA and HSA, but contributions to the MSA will reduce contribution limits to the HSA plan. A participant may roll over a preexisting MSA into an HSA plan.
2. HSA plans allow qualifying individuals with high-deductible health insurance plans to make tax-deductible cash contributions (above-the-line deductions). The 2011 contribution limits are $3,050 for single coverage and $6,150 for family coverage.
3. HSA funds can be used to reimburse the individual tax free for qualifying medical expenses
4. If an individual makes withdrawals for expenses other than qualifying medical expenses, the amount will be subject to income tax and a 20% penalty. The 20% penalty does not apply to withdrawals after age 65.
5. Earnings generated by the plan are not taxable, and distributions from an HSA used to pay medical expenses are excludable from taxable income
6. If the employer makes the contributions, they are excluded from the employee's income

VIII. PERSONAL AND DEPENDENCY EXEMPTIONS

A. PERSONAL EXEMPTIONS

1. An individual may claim a personal exemption for himself
2. An individual may also claim a personal exemption for a spouse if a joint return is filed
3. The personal exemption amount is $3,700 for 2011

B. DEPENDENCY EXEMPTIONS

1. A taxpayer can claim an additional exemption for each individual who qualifies as a dependent of the taxpayer
2. Per Tax Code, a dependency exemption can be claimed if an individual is either a qualifying child or qualifying relative of the taxpayer
   a. Qualifying child—a taxpayer may claim an individual as a dependent if the individual satisfies all of the following requirements
      1.) The individual must meet one of the following relationships
         a.) Child, stepchild, foster child, or adopted child of the taxpayer
         b.) Brother, sister, stepbrother, or stepsister of the taxpayer
         c.) Descendants of any of the individuals listed above
      2.) The individual must live with the taxpayer for more than half of the taxable year
      3.) The individual must pass an age test (meet one of the following)
         a.) Individual is under age 19 at the close of the tax year
         b.) Individual is a full-time student and under age 24 at the close of the tax year
         c.) Individual is totally and permanently disabled at any time during the tax year regardless of age
      4.) The individual must not have provided more than half of his own support during the tax year
      5.) The individual cannot claim any other individual as a dependent
      6.) The individual may not file a joint return for the tax year (unless the only reason a return was filed was to obtain a refund of tax withheld)
      7.) The individual generally must also be a US citizen, US national, or resident of the United States, Canada, or Mexico
      8.) The individual must also be younger than the taxpayer claiming the exemption

b. Qualifying relative—a taxpayer may claim an individual as a dependent if the individual satisfies all of the following requirements

1.) The individual is not a qualifying child of the taxpayer or of any other taxpayer for the tax year, as defined previously

2.) The individual must satisfy one of the following two requirements

a.) Bears a specified relationship to the taxpayer, including parent, in-law, niece, nephew, aunt, or uncle

b.) Is unrelated to the taxpayer but the individual resided in the taxpayer's principal home during the tax year

3.) The individual's gross income for the year must be less than the exemption amount

4.) The taxpayer provides over one-half of the individual's support for the tax year

5.) The individual cannot claim any other individual as a dependent

6.) The individual may not file a joint return for the tax year (unless the only reason a return was filed was to obtain a refund of tax withheld)

7.) The individual generally must also be a US citizen, US national, or resident of the United States, Canada, or Mexico

3. As long as all the tests are met, a dependency exemption can be taken for a person who dies during the year, without a reduction

4. Eligible taxpayers are generally free to agree among themselves who will claim a dependency exemption for an individual who can be claimed by more than one taxpayer

a. Only one person can claim a dependency exemption for an individual (exemption cannot be prorated)

b. If more than one individual files a return claiming the same individual as a dependent, the tiebreaker rules apply

If:	**Then the child will be treated as the qualifying child of the:**
only one of the persons is the child's parent	parent
both persons are the child's parents	parent with whom the child lived for the longer period; if the child lived with each parent for the same amount of time, the child will be treated as the qualifying child of the parent with the highest AGI
neither of the persons is the child's parent	person with the highest AGI

c. For tax years beginning after 2008

1.) Individual who satisfies the uniform definition of a qualifying child must be:

a.) younger than the individual claiming the child; or

b.) permanently or totally disabled

2.) If no parent claims the qualifying child as a dependent, another taxpayer may claim the child if:

a.) the taxpayer is otherwise eligible to claim the child as an exemption; and

b.) the taxpayer has a higher AGI than any parent eligible to claim the child

5. A child is treated as a dependent of both parents

a. For the purpose of employer-provided benefits

1.) Medical expense reimbursements

2.) Use of certain no-additional-cost services or employer-provided discounts by the employee's child

3.) Distributions from HSAs and Archer MSAs for the child's qualified medical expenses

b. Custodial spouse does not have to release the dependency exemption to other spouse

c. For taxpayers who are under a decree of divorce or separate maintenance, legally separated under a written agreement, or live apart at all times for at least six months of the calendar year and are the parents of a child who:

1.) receives over one-half of her support from the child's parents;

2.) is in the custody of one or both of the parents for more than one-half of the calendar year; and

3.) qualifies as a qualifying child or qualifying relative of one of the child's parents

EXAMPLES

- Erin and Brian, both age 50, filed a joint return for the current year. They provided all the support for their 19-year-old unmarried daughter, who had no income and lived with them the entire year. Their 23-year-old son, a full-time student at a university, had $5,000 of income and provided 70% of his own support.

  Three exemptions are allowed: two personal exemptions for Erin and Brian and one dependency exemption for their daughter. No exemption is allowed for their son. Although the gross income test is waived, they did not meet the support test for him.
- Dennis, age 50, filed a joint return with his wife, Kelly, age 24. Their son, Derek, was born December 16 of the taxable year. Dennis provided 60% of the support for his 73-year-old widowed mother until May 1, when she died. His mother's only income was from Social Security benefits totaling $4,000.

  The couple is entitled to four exemptions—Dennis, Kelly, their son Derek, and Dennis's mother. An exemption is allowed for a dependent who was alive during any part of the taxable year. Dennis's mother's Social Security income is excluded from gross income; thus, it is not considered in applying the gross income test.
- Andre provided more than one-half of the support for his cousin, his niece, and his foster parent. None of them lived in Andre's household. None of these relatives had any income, nor did any of them file an individual or joint return. All of the relatives are US citizens. Of the potential dependents listed, only the niece is a qualifying relative.
- Claudia, age 15, has lived with her older sister, Nancy, age 19, for the past two years. There are no parents living in the home. Nancy provides all of Claudia's support. Nancy may claim Claudia as a dependent on her income tax return and also for the earned income credit, if it applies.
- Gary and Lori are the parents of Neil, age 6. They provide 100% of Neil's support. Under the divorce agreement entered into in 2007, Lori is the custodial parent. Gary is required by the same agreement to provide health insurance for Neil through his employer. Even though Lori may claim Neil as a dependent on her income tax return and Gary may not, Gary may designate Neil as a dependent child for medical insurance purposes.

C. STANDARD DEDUCTION WHEN CLAIMED AS A DEPENDENT

1. The standard deduction of a person who may be claimed as a dependent of another is limited to the greater of:
   a. $950 (for 2011); or
   b. earned income plus $300
   c. Dependent's standard deduction cannot be greater than the regular standard deduction
   d. No personal exemption is allowed

EXAMPLE Andrea is claimed as a dependent on her parents' return. She earned $2,900 as a runner for her Dad's law firm. She also has $2,000 in dividend and interest income. Andrea's standard deduction is $3,200 ($2,900 + 300). She receives no personal exemption because she is claimed as a dependent on someone else's return.

D. PHASEOUT OF PERSONAL AND DEPENDENCY EXEMPTIONS

For 2011, under the EGTRRA sunset, the phaseout for personal and dependency exemptions returns. The total amount of the exemptions is reduced by 2% for each $2,500 ($1,250 for MFS). AGI exceeds the thresholds (see Exhibit 4).

IX. TAX DETERMINATION

A. CALCULATION OF NET TAXES PAYABLE/REFUND DUE

1. Estimated taxes paid, previously withheld taxes, and tax credits are subtracted from tax liability to reduce the tax due dollar for dollar. Tax credits include earned income credit, credit for child and dependent care expenses, credit for the elderly, and foreign tax credit.
2. An underpayment penalty will apply if an insufficient amount has been paid. See the Required Tax Payments in Section III (B) for ways to avoid the penalty.

B. KIDDIE TAX

1. The kiddie tax applies to unearned income of
   a. A dependent child who has not attained age 19 before the close of the tax year or a full-time student who has not attained age 24 before the close of the tax year
      1.) An individual will be considered a full-time student if she is a full-time student for at least five months of the taxable year
      2.) The kiddie tax will not apply to individuals age 18 (or students age 19–23) if their earned income for the taxable year exceeds one-half of their support
2. Unearned income above $1,900 is taxed at the parents' highest marginal rate. The net unearned income is the amount taxed at the parents' rate, computed as follows:

   Total unearned income

   Less $950 for 2011

   Less the greater of:

   - $950 for 2011; or
   - the amount of the allowable itemized deductions directly connected with the production of unearned income

   Equals net unearned income
3. Generally, the total unearned income will be reduced by $1,900 (2011) in arriving at the amount subject to kiddie tax (taxation at the parents' tax rate)

EXAMPLE Ann is age 14 and earned $5,600 from babysitting in 2011. She also had interest of $2,000 from her savings account. Ann's net unearned income is:

$2,000	Gross unearned income
(1,900)	Kiddie tax threshold
$100	Net unearned income taxed at parents' rate

Ann's taxable income is:

$5,600	Babysitting
2,000	Savings account interest
$7,600	Gross income
(5,800)	Standard deduction (earned income plus $300 but limited to $5,800)
(0)	Personal exemption
$1,800	Taxable income

Of the $1,800 in taxable income, $100 ($2,000 – $1,900) is taxed at her parents' highest rate and the remaining $1,700 ($1,800 – $100) is taxed at Ann's rate. In 2011, dividend income is taxed at the taxpayer's ordinary income tax rate. Under the kiddie tax rules, that would be the child's ordinary income tax rate for the child's portion and the parent's ordinary income tax rate for the portion taxable at the parent's rate.

X. FILING CONSIDERATIONS

A. FILING STATUS

1. There are five filing status categories
   a. Single
   b. Married filing jointly
   c. Married filing separately
   d. Head of household
   e. Qualifying widow(er) with dependent child (also called surviving spouse)
2. Single
   a. An unmarried, separated, or divorced individual who does not qualify for another status must file as a single taxpayer
   b. Exceptions—example
      1.) Abandoned spouses who live apart may be able to use the more advantageous head of household rate schedule
   c. Marital status is determined as of the last day of the tax year, except when a spouse dies during the year, in which case the survivor may file as married filing jointly
3. Married filing jointly or separately
   a. Married individuals are allowed to file joint returns or separate returns
   b. Separate returns
      1.) Each spouse reports only his own income, exemptions, deductions, and credits
      2.) Each spouse must use the tax rate for married persons filing separately
   c. The tax law places limits on married taxpayers filing separately
      1.) For example, they cannot take the credit for child and dependent care expenses, the earned income credit, or any education credits
      2.) If one spouse itemizes, the other generally should itemize because the standard deduction would be reduced to zero (some exceptions apply)
   d. Advantageous for married persons to file jointly because the combined amount of tax is generally lower
      1.) Special situations may exist that result in a lower married filing separate tax liability (e.g., spouse with low income has high medical expenses)
      2.) Calculate the tax under both assumptions to determine the most advantageous filing status
4. Head of household
   a. Unmarried individuals who maintain a household for a qualifying person for more than one-half of the tax year
   b. Rate schedule ranks between the joint and the single return tax rate schedules

c. Taxpayer must pay more than half the cost of maintaining a household for a qualifying person

d. The household must be the qualifying person's principal home

e. Qualifying persons

1.) Child, grandchild, stepchild, or adopted child

a.) A single child does not have to be a dependent

b.) A married child must qualify as a dependent unless the child is claimed by the noncustodial parent under a written court agreement

2.) Any other person that the taxpayer is entitled to claim as a dependent

3.) Parents may be claimed as the qualifying person for head of household even when not a member of the household

a.) If the taxpayer maintains a separate home for parents and pays more than half the cost of upkeep on that home or pays more than half the cost of a rest home or home for the elderly, the taxpayer may claim head of household filing status

EXHIBIT 13: Qualifying Persons

Qualifying Person	Claimed as a Dependent	Must Live in Taxpayer's Home More Than Half of the Year
Single Child	No	Yes
Married Child	Yes[1]	Yes
Other Relative	Yes	Yes
Parents	Yes	No[2]

[1] Qualifies as a dependent unless noncustodial spouse claims the exemption

[2] Taxpayer pays more than half of the cost of separate home or elder care home

5. Qualifying widow(er) (also called surviving spouse) with dependent child

a. A taxpayer with a deceased spouse will file as married filing jointly with two personal exemptions in the year of the death of the spouse

b. Taxpayer may be eligible to use qualifying widow(er) with dependent child as the filing status for two years following the year of death of a spouse

1.) Entitles the taxpayer to use joint return tax rates with one personal exemption and the highest standard deduction amounts (if taxpayer does not itemize deductions)

2.) Cannot file a joint return or claim an exemption for the deceased spouse

c. Eligibility rules for filing as a qualifying widow(er) with dependent child

1.) Must meet all of the following tests

a.) The taxpayer was entitled to file a joint return with his spouse for the year his spouse died (it does not matter whether the taxpayer actually filed a joint return) b.) Did not remarry before the end of the tax year in question

c.) Has a child, stepchild, adopted child, or foster child who qualifies as a dependent for that tax year

d.) Paid more than half the cost of upkeep of the main home for the taxpayer and the child for the entire year except for temporary absences

> **EXAMPLE** John's wife died in Year 1. John has not remarried. During Year 2 and Year 3 he continued to maintain a home for himself and his dependent child. For Year 1, he was entitled to file a joint return. For Year 2 and Year 3, he may file as a qualifying widower with a dependent child. After Year 3, he may file as head of household if he qualifies (otherwise, he would file as single).

B. FILING REQUIREMENTS

1. The following individuals are not required to file unless their income is equal to or exceeds their exemption amount plus the applicable standard deductions
   a. Single individual
   b. Head of household
   c. Surviving spouse
2. Individuals who file as married filing jointly are not required to file unless their combined gross income equals or exceeds the basic standard deduction, plus twice the exemption amount. Individuals who file as married filing separately must file if their income equals or exceeds the exemption amount.
   a. See Exhibit 14 for 2011 required filing levels
3. Filing requirements for dependents—if someone claims the taxpayer as a dependent, filing requirements for the dependent are controlled by the amount and type of income of the dependent. See Section VIII(C): Standard Deduction When Claimed as a Dependent.

Type of Income	Filing Required If Income Equals or Exceeds
Earned income only	Standard deduction including additional standard deduction for age and blindness
Unearned income only	Standard deduction[1] including additional standard deduction amounts for age and blindness
Earned income and unearned income	Standard deduction[2] including additional standard deduction amounts for age and blindness

[1] With no earned income, the standard deduction would be $950 (2011) plus any additional amounts.

[2] Greater of $950 (2011) or earned income plus $300 plus any additional amounts.

EXHIBIT 14: Filing Levels (Required to File)

Filing Status	2011 Gross Income
Single	
Under 65	$9,500
65 or older	$10,950
Married Filing Joint Return	
Both spouses under 65	$17,050
One spouse 65 or older	$18,200
Both spouses 65 or older	$19,350
Married Filing Separate Return	
All—whether or not 65 or older	$3,700
Head of Household	
Under 65	$12,200
65 or older	$13,650
Qualifying Widow(er)	
Under 65	$13,350
65 or older	$14,500

NOTE: The additional standard deduction for age is taken into account, but the additional standard deduction for blindness is not.

EXAMPLES

- In 2011, a single individual who is claimed by a parent as a dependent has earned income of only $3,800. No return would be required because the income is less than the standard deduction amount ($5,800).
- In 2011, a single, blind individual who is claimed by a parent as a dependent has unearned income amounting to only $1,200. The dependent does not need to file because gross income does not exceed $2,400 [$950 + 1,450 (additional standard deduction for blindness)].
- In 2011, a single individual claimed as a dependent by a parent has earned income of $2,000 and unearned income of $1,800 (total income—$3,800). This taxpayer must file because the earned and unearned income total is more than the standard deduction of $2,300 (earned income plus $300).

4. Selecting the proper form—depending on the level of complexity, an individual taxpayer may file a Form 1040, Form 1040A, or Form 1040EZ
   a. IRS Form 1040EZ is the most user-friendly of all three income tax forms and may be used if a number of requirements apply. The most important of these filing requirements include the following.
      1.) Taxpayer income is derived solely from wages, salaries, or tips
      2.) Taxable income is less than $100,000 annually
      3.) No dependents are claimed
      4.) No adjustments to income are claimed
   b. IRS Form 1040A is used where the taxpayer does not meet all of the requirements to file IRS Form 1040EZ and if:
      1.) the only adjustments to taxpayer income are for deductible contributions to an IRA and the student loan interest deduction;
      2.) deductions are not itemized; and
      3.) only certain tax credits are claimed.
   c. An individual taxpayer who does not meet the requirements for either Form 1040EZ or 1040A (and has sufficient income) must file using the longer IRS Form 1040

C. RETURN DUE DATE

1. Return is due on the 15th day of the fourth month after the end of the tax year. If this date falls on a weekend or holiday, return is due the next business day.
2. A six-month extension of time to file can be requested on Form 4868
3. If taxpayer overpays taxes and wants a refund, a claim must be filed by the later of three years from the date the return was filed (if filed early, return is counted as filed on the due date) or two years from the date tax was last paid

D. DECEDENT'S FINAL INCOME TAX RETURN

1. A final income tax return must be filed for a decedent for the portion of the tax year that ends on the date of the decedent's death
2. The return is due on the filing date that would have applied if death had not occurred. This would be April 15 for a calendar-year individual. Typically, the final income tax return will be filed by the executor or the administrator of the estate.
3. The surviving spouse may file a joint return with the decedent if the following conditions are met
   a. An executor or administrator has not been appointed by the time the joint return is prepared
   b. An executor or administrator has not been appointed before the extended due date of the tax return for the surviving spouse
   c. The decedent did not previously file a tax return for the tax year

4. Income inclusion
   a. Cash-basis taxpayer—only income actually or constructively received up to the date of death is included in the decedent's final income tax return
      1.) This amount could include any uncashed payroll or dividend checks
   b. Accrual-basis taxpayer—generally, only income accrued up to the date of death is included in the decedent's final income tax return
5. Deductions
   a. Cash-basis taxpayer—the expenses the decedent paid before death are deductible on the final income tax return
   b. Accrual-basis taxpayer—the expenses for which the decedent was liable before death, regardless of whether the expenses were paid, are deductible on the final income tax return
   c. Standard deduction and personal exemption amounts are allowed in full

XI. DEDUCTIONS AND LOSSES

A. CLASSIFICATION OF DEDUCTIBLE EXPENSES—FOR AGI VERSUS FROM AGI

1. Deductions for AGI
   a. Often referred to as above-the-line deductions
   b. Include expenses relating to a trade or business, alimony paid, 50% of self-employment tax paid, capital loss deduction, interest penalty for early withdrawal of savings, deductible IRA contributions, student loan interest, and moving expenses
2. Itemized deductions are deductions from AGI
   a. Often referred to as below-the-line deductions
   b. Include charitable contributions, medical expenses, mortgage interest, taxes paid, casualty losses, and unreimbursed employee business expenses
   c. Also known as Schedule A itemized deductions
3. Section 162 allows deductions for expenses incurred in a trade or business. Section 212 allows deductions for expenses incurred in connection with investment activities.
   a. Most expenses incurred in a trade or business are deductions for AGI (above the line). Investment expenses are deductions from AGI (with the exception of expenses incurred to produce rents and royalties).
   b. To be deductible in either case, both Section 162 and Section 212 expenses must have a profit motive
4. Reporting procedures
   a. Deductions for AGI are reported on the front (page 1) of Form 1040 before the calculation of AGI
   b. Deductions from AGI are itemized deductions reported on Schedule A

B. ORDINARY, NECESSARY, AND REASONABLENESS REQUIREMENTS

1. Ordinary and necessary requirement
   a. To be deductible, expenses must be ordinary and necessary
   b. Expenses are deemed necessary if a prudent person would make the same expenditure in the same situation
   c. Expenses are ordinary if it is normal or customary to make the expenditure (not capital)
2. Reasonableness requirement
   a. Requirement is typically associated with compensation amounts and particularly with closely held corporations
   b. C corporation—if a distribution from a C corporation is classified as a dividend, the distribution will be double taxed, once to the corporation and once to the recipient-shareholder

1.) If the IRS determines that compensation paid by a corporation to a shareholder is unreasonably high, the excess compensation will be classified as a dividend (double taxed)

2.) The burden of proof is on the company. There is no standard formula to determine reasonableness of compensation.

3.) In determining reasonableness, the IRS will consider the following factors:

a.) Size of the company

b.) Duties of the employee receiving the compensation

c.) Qualifications of the employee

d.) Salaries for similar executives

e.) Conflicts of interest

f.) Salary of shareholder compared to gross income of company

g.) Evidence of a consistent compensation plan

c. S corporation—a distribution to a shareholder is generally treated as a tax-free return of capital

1.) S corporation shareholder would probably desire a distribution from an S corporation rather than a salary, which is subject to FICA taxes

2.) If the IRS determines that compensation is unreasonably low, the IRS will likely reclassify any excess of the distribution as salary

3.) The salary will be subject to FICA taxes

C. DEDUCTIONS AND LOSSES—TIMING OF EXPENSE RECOGNITION

1. Taxpayer method of accounting
   a. Two most common are the cash method and the accrual method
   b. A cash-basis taxpayer generally receives a deduction when the expense has been paid
   c. An accrual-basis taxpayer generally receives a deduction when the expense is incurred
2. Cash-basis requirements
   a. Deduction is allowed only when paid
   b. Income is not recognized until cash is constructively received
   c. Capital outlays (even if made in cash) are not current deductions except as depreciation, amortization, or depletion
   d. Prepaid expenses are required to be capitalized and amortized only if the life of the asset extends more than one taxable year after the year of payment

3. Accrual-basis requirements
    a. Takes a deduction or claims income when all the events have occurred to create the taxpayer's liability or right to receive income and the amount of the liability or income can be determined with reasonable accuracy (all events test)
    b. Economic performance test must also be satisfied for deductions

D. DISALLOWED DEDUCTIONS

1. The IRC and the courts deny deductions for activities that are contrary to public policy
    a. Fines and bribes are not deductible
    b. Bribes, kickbacks, and other illegal payments are disallowed
    c. Expenses relating to the trafficking of controlled substances (i.e., drugs) are not allowed
2. Political contributions—political contributions are not deductible, whether paid to political action committees or directly to political candidates
3. Lobbying activities
    a. No deduction allowed
    b. Exceptions allowed for local, monitoring, and de minimis (< $2,000 annually)
4. Disallowance of deductions for capital expenditures—no current deduction is available for buildings, betterments, or permanent improvements made to property
    a. Must capitalize and depreciate over an appropriate period
    b. Can be depreciated using ACRS (pre-1987) or MACRS (post-1986) tax depreciation methods
    c. The asset must have an ascertainable life (e.g., land has none and, therefore, is not depreciable)
    d. Intangible assets are amortized over 15 years (including goodwill)
5. Personal expenditures—deductions of this nature are only deductible if a section of the IRC specifically allows it
6. Expenditures made on behalf of others
    a. No deduction is allowed for expenditures that benefit another taxpayer, but an exception is allowed for payment of medical expenses. Medical expenditures for a spouse or dependents are deductible by a taxpayer.

EXAMPLE Fred paid the following expenses for his dependent son during the current year:

Principal payment on son's automobile loan	$15,000
Payment of interest on above loan	$1,500
Payment of son's medical expenses	$4,000
Payment of son's property taxes (ad valorem)	$1,000

The $4,000 in medical expenses are deductible by Fred. The other items are not incurred for the taxpayer's benefit or are a result of the taxpayer's legal obligation and are not tax deductible.

7. Tax-exempt income-related expenses and interest—if income is tax exempt, taxpayer cannot deduct expenses or interest related to that income

E. LIMITED DEDUCTIONS (COMPENSATION, POTENTIAL START-UP/ORGANIZATION OF A NEW BUSINESS, HOBBY LOSSES, AND VACATION RENTAL HOMES)

1. Executive compensation—maximum of $1 million on the deductibility of executive compensation of large, publicly held corporations
   a. Excluded from this cap are commissions, performance-based bonuses, tax-qualified retirement contributions, and payments excluded from gross income
   b. Other exceptions are determined by Congressional legislation
2. Potential start-up/organization expenses related to a new business
   a. If a taxpayer investigates a business that is similar to the one he is already in, the expenses are deductible whether or not he acquires the business
   b. If a taxpayer investigates a business that is a new line of business and acquires the business, up to $5,000 of expenses can be deducted immediately. Remaining amounts may be amortized over no less than 180 months.
   c. Any expenses over $50,000 reduce the $5,000 deduction amount dollar for dollar
   d. If business is not acquired by the taxpayer, the expenses are nondeductible

	Taxpayer Already in a Similar Business	Taxpayer Not Already in Similar Business
Taxpayer acquires the business	Expenses currently deductible	Deduct $5,000 immediately and capitalize remaining costs and amortize over at least a 180-month period. Expenses in excess of $50,000 reduce the $5,000 deduction dollar for dollar.
Taxpayer does not acquire business	Expenses currently deductible	Not deductible

> **EXAMPLE** Kristin, a calendar-year, cash-basis taxpayer, owns and operates furniture rental outlets in Georgia. She wants to expand to other states. During the current year, she spends $20,000 investigating furniture stores in Alabama and $12,000 investigating stores in Florida. She acquires the Alabama stores but not the stores in Florida. Because she is already in the business, the expenses in both Alabama and Florida are deductible.

3. Losses incurred in hobby activities
   a. Classification as a hobby or business affects the deductibility of losses
   b. If an activity is deemed to be a hobby, losses incurred may not be fully deductible
   c. If an activity is a trade or business, the losses are deductible and can offset other taxpayer income
   d. IRS regulations and court cases specify the factors to be considered as follows
      1.) Whether the activity is conducted in a business-like manner
      2.) Expertise of the taxpayers or their advisers
      3.) Time and effort expended
      4.) Expectation that the assets of the activity will appreciate in value
      5.) Previous success of the taxpayer in the conduct of similar activities
      6.) History of income or losses from the activity
      7.) Relationship of profits earned to losses incurred
      8.) Financial status of the taxpayer (is there other income?)
      9.) Elements of personal pleasure or recreation in the activity
      10.) Conducting business professionally, time spent, regular hours, and so forth
   e. If the activity generated profits for three out of five years, the burden of proof is on the IRS rather than the taxpayer to prove that the activity is not a business
   f. Hobby income
      1.) reduced first by taxes and interest;
      2.) then by other non-capital-related expenses; and
      3.) then by expenses that affect basis
   g. Gross hobby income is reported on page 1 of Form 1040 (other income)
   h. Hobby expenses
      1.) Reported on Schedule A (itemized deductions) as miscellaneous itemized deductions subject to the 2% of AGI floor

d. Attribution rules (constructive ownership of stock)

1.) A taxpayer is treated as having constructive ownership of stock if owned directly or indirectly by related parties

a.) Related parties for this purpose are a spouse (not an ex-spouse or a legally separated spouse), children (adopted or natural), grandchildren, and parents

b.) Stock owned, directly or indirectly, by a trust is considered owned by the beneficiaries of the trust

c.) Stock owned by a beneficiary of a trust is also attributed as owned by the trust

d.) The attribution rules also apply to 50% or greater shareholders in a corporation relative to such stock owned by the corporation, and, in return, for the corporation for stock owned by a 50% or greater shareholder

> **EXAMPLE** On January 10, Year 1, Billy sold stock with a cost of $6,000 to his son, Patrick, for $4,000 (its fair market value). On July 31, Year 2, Patrick sold the same stock for $5,000 in a bona fide arms-length transaction.
>
> Neither Billy nor Patrick has a recognized gain or loss in either Year 1 or Year 2. Billy has a $2,000 realized loss in Year 1 but cannot recognize it. Billy forever loses the ability to take a deduction for the loss. Patrick has a realized gain of $1,000 in Year 2. He can reduce his gain by Billy's loss (up to the amount of gain). Patrick has no gain or loss in Year 2. The remaining $1,000 loss is no longer available to any taxpayer.

F. OTHER DEDUCTIONS AND LOSSES

1. Legal and accounting fees

a. When legal and accounting fees are incurred in connection with trade or business or for the production of rents and royalties, they are deductible for AGI

b. If these legal and accounting fees are incurred in the determination of any tax, they are deductible from AGI (as an itemized deduction)

c. Legal fees incurred for personal purposes are nondeductible

d. Legal fees related to the acquisition of an asset are added to the basis of the property

2. Worthless securities

a. Securities must be completely worthless to be deducted

b. Losses are deemed to be capital losses occurring on the last day of the year in which they become worthless, thereby creating increased potential for long-term capital loss treatment (net capital loss deduction remains limited to $3,000 per year)

3. Small business stock (Section 1244—applies to losses only)

a. Generally any security loss is capital in nature, but Section 1244 allows ordinary loss treatment if the loss is sustained by an individual who acquires the securities directly from the corporation (which must meet certain requirements)

b. Section 1244 losses are limited to $50,000 annually ($100,000 for joint filers)

   1.) Any losses in excess of the limits are capital losses

c. In order to qualify for Section 1244 treatment, the corporation must receive less than $1 million in capital for stock at time of issue

d. Section 1244 applies only to losses on the investment, not to gains

EXAMPLES

- Tom, a single taxpayer, owns Section 1244 stock he purchased three years ago for $80,000. This year, he sold all of the Section 1244 stock for $10,000, incurring a loss of $70,000. He had no other investment transactions for the year.

  Tom is single, so the first $50,000 of the loss on the Section 1244 stock will be treated as ordinary loss. The remaining $20,000 ($70,000 – $50,000) loss will be treated as a capital loss, of which Tom can currently deduct $3,000. The remaining capital loss of $17,000 can be carried forward.

- On October 15, Year 1, Kurt purchased stock in Tech Corporation (the stock is not small business stock) for $2,000. On June 15, Year 2, the stock became worthless.

  Kurt will have a $2,000 long-term capital loss. Worthless securities are treated as becoming worthless on the last day of the tax year; therefore, it is a long-term capital loss even though his actual holding period was only eight months. If the stock had been Section 1244 stock, Kurt would have had a $2,000 ordinary loss.

4. Bad debts

a. Specific charge-off method

   1.) Specific charge-off method is usually required, meaning the bad debt must be identified by the taxpayer; the deduction cannot be for general reserves against bad debt

   2.) Deductions are only allowed in year of worthlessness

   3.) If a previously deducted bad debt is later collected, income is recognized only if a tax benefit was received

b. Business bad debts

   1.) Business bad debts are sales or revenues (accounts receivable) on credit that later become worthless.

   2.) A deduction is only allowed if the income from the receivable was previously included in income (i.e., if accrual basis because income was reported at time of service; not for cash basis because no payment means income was never reported)

   3.) There must be an identifiable relationship between the creation of the debt and the trade or business

   4.) Deduction is allowed when business debts become partially or wholly worthless

   5.) Business bad debts are deductible as an ordinary loss in year incurred

c. Nonbusiness (personal) bad debts

   1.) Must be wholly worthless

   2.) Debt not related to the taxpayer's trade or business

3.) Always considered short-term capital losses

4.) Borrowed funds may be used for any purpose (because the deduction relates to the lender, not the borrower)

Type of Debt	Deduction
Business—partial or whole	Ordinary loss in year incurred
Nonbusiness—wholly worthless	Short-term capital loss in year incurred
Nonbusiness—partially worthless	None

EXAMPLES

- XYZ, Inc., is an accrual-basis taxpayer. XYZ uses the accounts receivable aging approach to calculate its accounting allowance for bad debts. The following information related to bad debts is available for the current year.

Credit sales	$450,000
Collections on credit sales	$375,000
Amount added to the allowance account	$60,000
Beginning balance in the allowance account	$25,000
Bad debts written off in the current year	$32,000

The tax deduction for bad-debt expense for XYZ, Inc., for the current year is $32,000. Only the specific charge-off method can be used. Allowances for estimated expenses are not allowed for tax purposes.

- Bob, a CPA, files his tax return using the cash method. Bob billed a client $4,500 for the following professional services:

Estate planning	$3,000
Personal tax return preparation	$1,000
Compilation of business financial statements	$500

No part of the $4,500 was ever paid. The client declared bankruptcy, and the $4,500 obligation became totally uncollectible. No loss is allowed for Bob; the indebtedness was never taken into income because Bob was a cash-basis taxpayer.

5. Unpaid loans between related parties
   a. Bona fide loan or a gift?
   b. To be a loan, there must be an enforceable obligation to pay a specific amount of money
   c. Other factors taken under consideration by the IRS are collateral, collection efforts, intent, interest paid, and so forth
6. Loss of deposits in insolvent financial institutions
   a. Loss of deposits may be deducted as personal casualty losses instead of nonbusiness bad debts, but they are then subject to 10% AGI limit and $100 floor
   b. This may be elected only by qualified individuals (i.e., not >1% owners, relatives, or officers)
   c. Amount of loss equals basis less amount to be received

7. Business casualty losses or held-for-production-of-income casualty losses
    a. The identifiable event must be sudden, unexpected, or unusual
    b. Losses related to business or trade property are deductible for AGI
    c. Not subject to the $100 or 10% AGI floors to which individuals are held
    d. Losses relating to property held for profit are not subject to the $100 and 10% floors and are deductible for AGI only if the property is held for rent or royalty
    e. If completely destroyed, the loss is the adjusted basis of the property
    f. If partially destroyed, the loss is the lesser of the adjusted basis or the decline in the FMV of the property (pre-event and post-event)
    g. For a discussion of personal casualty losses, see Section XV (F) Itemized Deductions
8. Ponzi scheme losses
    a. IRS issued Revenue Procedure 2009-20 and Revenue Ruling 2009-9 with guidance for victims of Ponzi-type investment schemes
    b. Deemed a theft loss when
        1.) the promoter was charged under state or federal law with the commission of fraud, embezzlement, or a similar crime that would meet the definition of theft; or
        2.) the promoter was the subject of a state or federal criminal complaint alleging the commission of such a crime, and
        3.) either there was some evidence of an admission of guilt by the promoter or a trustee was appointed to freeze the assets of the scheme
    c. Loss is a theft loss
        1.) Deductible as an itemized deduction
        2.) Not subject to $3,000 capital loss limit
        3.) Not a casualty loss subject to the $100 and 10% of AGI reductions
    d. Deductible in the year loss is discovered, except for amounts that may be reasonably recovered
    e. Amount of loss includes investor's unrecovered investment as well as any income from the investment reported on prior years' income tax returns
    f. A theft loss deduction that creates a net operating loss (NOL) for the taxpayer can be carried back and forward and generate a refund of taxes paid in other taxable years
    g. Revenue Procedure 2009-20 sets out a special rule for safe harbor deduction of the loss when it is difficult to determine possible recovery amounts
        1.) Each taxpayer must decide whether to use the safe harbor rules or deduct the loss as outlined in Revenue Procedure 2009-9
        2.) Guidance of tax and legal professionals is advised as the deduction can be very complicated

G. NET OPERATING LOSSES (NOLs)

1. The purpose of allowing NOLs is to create an equitable situation for cyclical businesses that might otherwise lose substantial money without receiving a tax benefit. The inequality would cause excessive average taxes for a business with irregular income and/or expenses when compared to a business with the same average income but with uniform income and expenses.
2. Carryback and carryover periods
   a. General rules—net operating losses may be carried back two years preceding the loss year and forward 20 years following the loss year
   b. Sequence of use of NOLs—the oldest is completely written off before using any of the more recent NOLs. Each loss is calculated and maintains its own integrity.
   c. Election to forgo carryback—this election is irrevocable. The election produces a tax advantage if the taxpayer was in a low tax bracket in earlier years and expects to be in a higher bracket in the carryforward years.

XII. DEPRECIATION, COST RECOVERY, AMORTIZATION, AND DEPLETION

A. INTRODUCTION

1. Taxpayers may recover the cost of certain assets used in trade or business through depreciation, amortization, or depletion
   a. Taxpayer must be the legal or equitable owner of the asset
   b. Property used for the production of income is ineligible for depreciation or Section 179 expensing (such as inventory)
2. The amount of annual recovery depends on the type of property, when it was acquired, and the elected method of recovery
3. Property eligible includes personalty, realty, and intangibles
4. The property must have a determinable useful life and be subject to wear and tear, decay or decline from natural causes, or obsolescence
5. The basis of an asset must be reduced by the cost recovery taken and by no less than the amount the taxpayer could have taken (allowable depreciation)
   a. In other words, if an individual does not take the depreciation allowed, she still must reduce the basis by the allowable depreciation
6. The simplest form of depreciation is straight-line depreciation
   a. Assumes that depreciation is uniform throughout the useful life of the asset
   b. The cost or adjusted basis of the asset, less the asset's residual or salvage value, is deducted in equal annual installments over the asset's useful life
      1.) SL = (Cost − residual value) ÷ useful life
   c. This method can be used under MACRS and ACRS depreciation methods, using the applicable recovery period instead of the useful life, and salvage value is not considered
   d. Must use the half-year convention

B. MODIFIED ACCELERATED COST RECOVERY SYSTEM (MACRS)

1. Under MACRS, tangible personalty is either 3-year, 5-year, 7-year, 10-year, 15-year, or 20-year property. The percentages are based on 200% declining balance for 10-year-and-less property and 150% declining balance for 15-year and 20-year property.
   a. Both 200% declining balance and 150% declining balance switch over to straight-line depreciation when it results in a larger deduction
   b. A half-year convention is used (half-year depreciation is allowed during the year placed in service, and a half-year depreciation is allowed in the year of disposition). However, the midquarter convention may apply (see following discussion).

2. Under MACRS, residential real estate has a 27.5-year life; nonresidential has a 39-year life
   a. Cost recovery percentages are calculated using straight line
   b. Midmonth convention is used (a half-month depreciation is allowed for month placed in service, and a half-month is allowed for month of disposition)
3. IRS tables provide the statutory percentages
   a. The statutory percentage is applied against the asset cost (no reduction for salvage value)
   b. The tables incorporate the conventions for the year or month placed in service
4. Midquarter convention
   a. In order to reduce the benefits of the half-year convention for property placed in service late in the year, the midquarter convention was developed
   b. If more than 40% of the personal property is placed in service during the last quarter of the year, the midquarter convention applies to all personal property assets placed in service that year
   c. In the first year of service, first-quarter assets get 10.5 months of depreciation, second-quarter assets get 7.5 months, third-quarter assets get 4.5 months, and fourth-quarter assets get 1.5 months
   d. The midquarter convention does not apply to real property

C. ELECTION TO EXPENSE ASSETS

1. Section 179 allows an annual write-off of the cost of tangible personal property used in a trade or business and placed in service during the current year
   a. The maximum write-off under Section 179 for tangible personal property other than sports utility vehicles and luxury autos is $500,000 for 2011
      1.) The $500,000 limit would apply to purchases of office equipment, business computers, and so forth
      2.) The $500,000 limit would also apply to vehicles with a gross vehicle weight in excess of 14,000 pounds
   b. The maximum write-off under Section 179 for sports utility vehicles is $25,000 for 2011
      1.) A sports utility vehicle is defined as any four-wheeled vehicle primarily designed for carrying passengers over public streets that has a gross vehicle weight in excess of 6,000 and not more than 14,000 pounds
      2.) An auto that weighs 6,000 pounds or less is subject to the luxury auto depreciation rules, discussed under Section E, Business Use of Listed Property
   c. Under the Small Business Jobs Act of 2010, a taxpayer may elect to treat up to $250,000 of qualified real property as Section 179 property for tax years that begin in 2010 and 2011
      1.) The taxable income limitation still applies

2.) Of the $500,000 limit on property placed in service in 2010 and 2011, qualified real property is limited to $250,000 annually

3.) There is no carryover of any amounts in excess of $250,000 to tax years beginning in 2012 and later

2. Annual limitations

a. If the total amount of property placed in service for a given year is above $2,000,000, the allowance is reduced dollar for dollar for any amount over $2,000,000. No carryover is allowed.

b. The amount of the deduction cannot exceed the taxable income from total trade or business of the taxpayer (carryforward is available)

EXAMPLES

- In 2011, Roth Corporation purchased and placed in service a piece of machinery costing $600,000. Assuming Roth had taxable income of $52,000 (without regard to Section 179 expense), the maximum Section 179 expense that can be taken is $52,000 ($500,000 is eligible, but this amount is limited to the taxable income) and $448,000 ($500,000 – $52,000) will be carried forward to 2012 and can only be deducted in 2012 to the extent that there is taxable income.
- In 2011, Lewis Corporation purchased $20,000 of new equipment and had taxable income (without regard to Section 179 expense) of $200,000. Section 179 expense deduction of $20,000 can be taken in 2011. This is under the $500,000 annual limit.

3. Effect on adjusted taxable basis

a. The adjusted taxable basis of the property is reduced by the amount of the Section 179 deduction taken as adjusted for the property placed in service limitation and is not adjusted for the income limitation

EXAMPLE The adjusted taxable basis of the property acquired by Roth in the previous example is:

Year 2011 = $600,000 (purchase price) – 500,000 (Section 179 limit) = $100,000 for equipment purchased.

EXAMPLE In 2011, Berry Corp. purchased and placed in service a machine to be used in its manufacturing operations. This machine cost $2,090,000. What portion of the cost may Berry elect to treat as an expense rather than as a capital expenditure, assuming net taxable income of $4 million?

Maximum allowable Section 179 expense for 2011	$500,000
Reduction ($2,090,000 – $2,000,000)	(90,000)
Allowed Section 179 expense	$410,000

Cost of property	$2,090,000
Section 179 expense	(410,000)
Adjusted tax basis of property	$1,680,000*

*Ignoring any depreciation allowable

D. REPAIRS VERSUS CAPITAL EXPENDITURES

1. The cost of repairing business property is currently deductible as a business expense. A repair could include the following
   a. An incidental expense that does not materially add to the value of the property
   b. An incidental expense that does not appreciably prolong the life of the property
   c. An expense that maintains the property in its normal operating state
2. If a cash outlay is considered a capital expenditure, the cash outlay is not currently deductible. Instead, the cost must be capitalized and depreciated over the property's useful life. A capital expenditure could include the following
   a. Expenditures that materially add to the value of the property
   b. Expenditures that substantially prolong the property's useful life
   c. Expenditures as part of a general plan of renovating, improving, or altering the property

> **EXAMPLE** Tom Hall operates Hall's Limo, a limousine service. Tom occasionally incurs expenses for the upkeep of his limousines. These expenses, which include items such as spark plugs, oil changes, and labor, would be considered repair and maintenance expenses because the expenses do not significantly prolong a limousine's useful life. However, if Tom replaced the transmission at a cost of $2,400, the expense would be considered a capital improvement.

E. BUSINESS USE OF LISTED PROPERTY

Listed property includes passenger automobiles, entertainment assets, computers, and phones. If the business usage of listed assets is greater than 50%, the taxpayer may use the statutory percentages for depreciation. If business usage is less than or equal to 50%, the taxpayer is limited to straight line.

1. Autos and other listed property used predominantly in business
   a. The percentage of business use must be above 50%. The 50% test is based on business use only and not on production of income. However, if the test is met, the cost recovery amount is based on both the business and production of income usage.
   b. The amount of cost recovery available is based on the percentage of the total use that is business related
   c. The amount of annual depreciation is subject to a limit. This limit is applied before the adjustment for business use percentage.
2. Autos and other listed property not used predominantly in business. (Note: only the portion used for business can be depreciated.)
   a. The depreciation for this property must be based on the straight-line method and the alternative depreciation system (ADS), which require a five-year period for autos
   b. The dollar limits previously described are still applicable
   c. If the property fails the 50% test, it must be depreciated using the straight-line method even if it later could pass the 50% test

3. Change from predominantly business use—if property initially passes the 50% test but later fails the test, the property is subject to cost recovery recapture. The amount of recapture is the amount of cost recovery claimed less the amount that could have been claimed if the straight-line method had been used from the beginning.
4. Leased automobiles—to prevent circumvention of the cost recovery rules by leasing, an annual inclusion amount (figured from IRS tables) is required to be reported as gross income. The amount reported is based on the fair market value, the number of days of use during the year, and the percentage of business versus personal use. The effect is to reduce the deduction of the lease payments by the inclusion amount.
5. Substantiation requirements—records must substantiate the taxpayer's claims pertaining to amount of expenditures, business purpose, and percentage use for business purposes

F. ALTERNATIVE DEPRECIATION SYSTEM (ADS)

Note that ADS must be used for alternative minimum tax adjustments, international asset use, tax-exempt entities, tax-exempt bond financed assets, and assets from certain discriminating countries for earnings and profit purposes

G. AMORTIZATION

1. Certain intangible assets are amortizable over 15 years
2. Section 197 assets include goodwill, trademarks, covenants not to compete, copyrights, and patents if they are used in a trade or business or for the production of income. Self-created intangibles are not considered amortizable assets under Section 197.

> **EXAMPLE** Maria acquired a business on July 1 of the current year. The purchase price included a copyright valued at $30,000. Maria can claim $1,000 of amortization in the current year. The annual amortization will be $30,000 ÷ 15 = $2,000. Recall, Maria held it only six months during the current year.

H. DEPLETION

1. Natural resources (except land) are subject to depletion. An owner of the resource is someone who acquires an economic interest and receives income from the resource. The owner is entitled to a deduction for AGI to recover his costs. The four types of expenditures are the cost of natural resources, the cost of intangible development, tangible asset costs, and operating costs.
2. Intangible drilling and development costs
   a. Two options for the taxpayer
      1.) Expense in year incurred
      2.) Capitalize and deplete
   b. After the election is made, all future expenditures of a similar nature are handled in the same way. Generally, the expense option is more advantageous.

3. Depletion methods
   a. Two depletion methods
      1.) Cost
      2.) Percentage
   b. This is an annual election, and usually the method yielding the larger deduction is chosen
   c. Cost depletion—the asset basis is divided by the estimated total number of recoverable units of the asset and then multiplied by the number of units sold (not produced) to determine the amount of the deduction for the year. If the estimated total number of recoverable units is inaccurate, future calculations are based on a revised estimate.
   d. Percentage depletion—a statutory percentage is applied to the gross income from the property (limited to 50% of the gross income). This method is unrelated to the cost or basis of the asset.
   e. Effect of intangible drilling costs on depletion—if the costs are capitalized, the basis of the property is increased and the cost depletion increases. If the costs are expensed, the 50% depletion limits may apply.

> **EXAMPLE** Cole owns a sulfur mine that had 100,000 total estimated tons when he purchased it for $2 million. In the current year, 20,000 tons were extracted and 18,000 tons were sold. The statutory percentage for sulfur is 22%. Gross income for the year was $1 million. His depletion deduction for the current year is $360,000.
>
> $$\text{Cost method: } \frac{\$2{,}000{,}000}{100{,}000} \times 18{,}000 = \$360{,}000$$
>
> Percentage method: 22% × 1,000,000 = $220,000
>
> Cole's depletion deduction will be $360,000 (the higher of the two methods).

XIII. PASSIVE ACTIVITY LOSSES

A. TAX SHELTER INVESTMENTS

1. Typically, tax shelter investments deferred or eliminated taxes for the investor. Before Congress curbed tax shelter abuse, these shelters allowed paper losses in excess of the amount of capital the investor provided because of the high expenses (depreciation, interest, development, and so forth) and low revenues in the early years of a project.
2. Two major changes in the IRC have significantly reduced the availability of tax shelters
   a. At-risk rules
   b. Passive activity loss limits
3. At-risk rules are applied before the passive activity loss limits

B. AT-RISK RULES

1. The maximum deductible loss for an activity is limited to the amount that the investor has at risk at the end of the current tax year (i.e., the potential economic loss)
2. The amount at risk is the total of the cash and property invested and the debt for which the investor is personally liable (typically referred to as recourse debt). The amount is adjusted annually on the basis of the taxpayer's share of taxable profit or deductible loss from the investment.
   a. Nonrecourse debt is a liability for which the partner has no risk of economic loss if the liability is not satisfied by the partnership (for example, a mortgage or loan secured solely by a lien on an asset owned by the partnership)
   b. For recourse debt, a limited partner cannot be allocated recourse liabilities in excess of that limited partner's capital contribution and future contribution obligations unless there is an agreement with the partnership to the contrary
   c. Total amount each partner has at risk is adjusted annually (like basis) by the taxpayer-investor's share of profit or loss from the activity
3. If a loss is disallowed because of at-risk rules, the loss can be carried forward and taken in the first year the at-risk amount becomes a positive amount (enough to absorb the loss)
4. Generally, when a passive activity interest is disposed of in a taxable transaction, any net passive loss first must be applied against income or gain from any other passive activities of the taxpayer
   a. Any loss in excess of the netting against passive income or gain is then reclassified as nonpassive and may be used to offset ordinary (nonpassive) income such as wages and interest income
   b. If it is a related party transaction, the loss may only be claimed when the related party disposes of the activity with an unrelated person. Abandonment is considered a fully taxable transaction.

> **EXAMPLE** In Year 1, Bob invested $50,000 for a 20% interest in a partnership in which he was a material participant during the year. The partnership incurred a loss, and Bob's share was $75,000.
>
> Bob has only $50,000 of capital at risk, so he cannot deduct more than $50,000 against his other income. Bob's nondeductible loss of $25,000 can be carried over and used when the at-risk provisions allow. If Bob has taxable income of $45,000 from the partnership in Year 2 and no other transactions that affect his at-risk amount, he can use all of the $25,000 loss carried over from Year 1. In this case, he would only recognize $20,000 of taxable income from the partnership in Year 2.

C. PASSIVE ACTIVITY LOSS LIMITS

1. Passive activity loss rules—passive losses may only be deducted against passive income
   a. Investors are prohibited from deducting passive losses against either active income (wages, salaries, and other employee compensation) or portfolio income (dividends, interest, and capital gains)
   b. Because active and portfolio income likely constitutes the majority, if not all, of an investor's income in any one year, the passive loss restrictions have effectively curtailed all tax-shelter investment activity conducted in the limited partnership form
2. Apply to the following
   a. Individuals
   b. Estates
   c. Trusts
   d. Closely held C corporations
   e. Personal service corporations (PSCs)
3. Passive activity loss rules divide all income into active, passive, and portfolio
4. Limit the deduction for passive losses to the amount of passive income (with exceptions for real estate activities)
   a. The limits are applied to closely held corporations to prevent an individual or business from incorporating solely to take advantage of passive losses
   b. Closely held corporations may offset passive losses against active income but not portfolio income
   c. The limits are applied to personal service corporations (PSCs) to prevent professionals from forming a PSC and using it to acquire investments that produce passive losses to deduct against active corporate profits
   d. A PSC is a corporation where the primary economic activity is the performance of personal services by the owners of the corporation

D. CLASSIFICATION OF INCOME AND LOSSES

1. Taxpayer must classify income and losses into active, passive, or portfolio
2. Passive loss limitations prevent the taxpayer from deducting any passive losses against active or portfolio income
3. Active income examples
   a. Wages, salaries, and other employee compensation
   b. Trade or business income when taxpayer is a material participant
   c. Intangible property income when taxpayer significantly contributed to the creation
   d. Qualified low-income housing project income
4. Portfolio income examples
   a. Interest, dividends, annuities, and royalties
   b. Gain or loss from disposition of property that produces portfolio income or is held for investment
5. An oil and gas activity that involves a working (not royalty) interest in any oil and gas property that a taxpayer owns directly, or through a general partnership, is not a passive activity
6. Limited partnerships
   a. For purposes of the passive activity loss rules, there are two types of limited partnerships:
      1.) Publicly traded partnership (PTP), also known as a master limited partnership (MLP)
      2.) Nonpublicly traded or privately offered limited partnership
   b. A publicly traded partnership (or MLP) is a partnership that is traded on an established securities exchange
   c. Losses from a nonpublicly traded limited partnership [or real estate limited partnerships (RELPs), because such partnerships are usually invested in real estate properties] may only be used to offset income from another nonpublicly traded limited partnership
      1.) This income does not have to be generated from the same nonpublicly traded limited partnership
      2.) Any RELP that generates passive income (also referred to as a passive income generator, or PIG), will suffice
      3.) A passive income loss generated from a RELP may offset income from a passive income generator, if indeed such an investment activity is available for purchase by the investor

E. PASSIVE ACTIVITIES DEFINED

1. Either of the following conditions creates a passive activity
   a. The taxpayer does not materially participate (except in oil and gas partnerships)
   b. The activity is a rental activity (even if the taxpayer does materially participate)

2. If the answer to any of the following is yes, the taxpayer is a material participant and the activity is not passive
   a. Does the taxpayer complete more than 500 hours of participation during the year?
   b. Does the individual's participation in the activity constitute substantially all of the participation in the activity of all individuals (including individuals who are not owners) for the year?
   c. Does the taxpayer participate for more than 100 hours, and is this amount equal to or more than any other participant in the activity?
   d. Is the activity a significant participation activity (i.e., more than 100 hours of participation), and does significant participation in all such activities exceed 500 hours?
   e. Did the taxpayer materially participate in the activity in at least 5 of the last 10 years?
   f. Is the activity a personal service activity, and did the taxpayer materially participate in the activity in any three previous years?
   g. Using the existing facts and circumstances, did the taxpayer participate on a regular, continuous, and substantial basis during the year (100 hours per year minimum)?
3. An oil or gas activity that involves a working interest that a taxpayer owns directly, or through an entity that does not limit the taxpayer's liability, is not a passive activity
   a. Losses can be applied against active and portfolio income
   b. This exception is applied on a well-by-well basis
4. Limited partners are not material participants because they are not allowed to participate in the management of the business and are therefore limited partnership interests, considered passive activities
5. Rental activities
   a. Unless excepted by the Code, all rental activities are deemed passive
      1.) Rental activities occur when payments are received for the use of tangible property
      2.) If an activity is excepted by the Code, it still must pass the material participation test to be considered active
   b. An activity is not rental under any of the following six conditions
      1.) The average customer use is seven days or less
      2.) The average customer use is more than seven days but not over 30 days, and the owner provides significant personal services
      3.) The owner also provides extraordinary services (rental period is irrelevant)
      4.) The rental activity is incidental to a nonrental activity of taxpayer (investment or trade/business)
      5.) The property is customarily made available during business hours for nonexclusive use by customers (e.g., golf course)
      6.) The property is used in a nonrental activity conducted by a partnership, S corporation, or joint venture where the owner has an interest

F. SPECIAL RULES FOR PUBLICLY TRADED PARTNERSHIPS

1. The partnership is traded on an established securities market or is readily tradable on a secondary market
2. Sometimes referred to as MLPs, or master limited partnerships
3. Losses from a publicly traded partnership
    a. Can only be used to offset income from that same publicly traded partnership
4. Losses from a publicly traded partnership that are disallowed can be carried forward and allowed as a deduction in a year when the same publicly traded partnership has net income or is disposed of

> **EXAMPLE** Dana purchased an interest in a nonpublicly traded partnership that had income in the current year of $15,000. She also purchased an interest in a master limited partnership with $20,000 of losses. Losses from a publicly traded partnership cannot offset income from any other limited partnership. So, the income of $15,000 from the nonpublicly traded limited partnership will be fully taxable to Dana this year, and the $20,000 loss will be disallowed (suspended) this year (and carried forward).

G. EXCEPTION FOR REAL ESTATE ACTIVITIES

1. Real estate trade or business
    a. Losses are not considered passive for certain real estate professionals, provided that:
        1.) real estate is greater than 50% of their personal services in all trades or businesses for the year; and
        2.) the taxpayer performs greater than 750 hours of service in real property trades or business in which the taxpayer materially participates
    b. Real estate professionals who meet the participation test listed previously will treat losses from real estate rental activities as nonpassive and can offset those losses against active and portfolio income
2. Real estate rental activities for non-real estate professionals
    a. Individuals can deduct up to $25,000 of rental real estate losses against active and portfolio income
    b. Two tests must be met to qualify for this exception
        1.) Active participation in the activity (makes management decisions in a bona fide sense, an easier hurdle to clear than material participation)
        2.) Ownership of 10% or more (in value) of all interests in the activity during the taxable year
    c. The $25,000 offset allowance is reduced by 50% of AGI in excess of $100,000 (complete phaseout at $150,000 AGI). Therefore, there is a loss of $1 for every $2 of AGI greater than $100,000. The loss is deducted from the $25,000 maximum available. Note: Two steps are required for this calculation:
        1.) Determine the maximum allowable loss (based on AGI)
        2.) Limit this calculated loss by the actual rental real estate losses incurred

3.) AGI is calculated by disregarding the following:

a.) Taxable Social Security and railroad retirement benefits

b.) The exclusion for qualified US savings bonds used for qualified higher education expenses

c.) The exclusion for employer adoption assistance

d.) The exclusion for passive activity income and losses on Form 8582, losses from publicly-traded partnerships, and rental real estate losses for real estate professionals

e.) Deductions attributed to domestic production activities, contributions to IRAs and pension plans, and one-half of self-employment taxes

f.) Deductions attributed to interest on student loans and higher education expenses

H. DISPOSITION OF PASSIVE ACTIVITIES/SUSPENDED LOSSES AND CARRYOVERS

1. The at-risk rules are applied before the passive loss rules. If a loss is not allowed because of the at-risk limitations, it is not a suspended loss under the passive loss rules. Rather, it is suspended under the at-risk rules.

EXAMPLE

- Ronnie, who earned a salary of $180,000, invested $30,000 for a 15% interest in a passive activity in the current year. Operations of the activity resulted in a loss of $300,000, of which Ronnie's share was $45,000. Therefore, $15,000 of Ronnie's loss is suspended under the at-risk rules, which leaves a potential deduction of $30,000. The $30,000 loss is suspended under the passive loss rules because Ronnie does not have any passive income.
- Larry has the following income and losses for the current year:

Salary for managing an S corporation	$50,000
Dividend income from ABC Company stock	$1,000
Loss from a 20% limited partnership interest in Realty Capital Partners, a limited partnership	($4,000)
Loss from a 10% interest in an S corporation, in which he works full time managing one of the branches	($3,000)

His AGI is calculated as follows:

Salary	$50,000
Dividend income	1,000
Limited partnership interest (passive loss cannot be deducted because limited partners are not material participants)	0
S corporation interest (works full time and is therefore a material participant)	(3,000)
AGI	$48,000

a. The passive activity loss limitation is not a permanent disallowance rule

1.) Disposition of the entire interest in a fully taxable transaction to an unrelated purchaser (not a related party), and suspended losses from that activity—including any losses incurred in the year of disposition, are generally deductible in full

2.) Disposition of a taxpayer's entire interest in a passive activity is a disposition of his interest in all entities that are engaged in the passive activity and, to the extent that the activity is owned in the sole proprietorship form, all of the assets used or created in that activity

3.) Disposition by gift does not trigger recognition of the suspended losses. Instead, the basis of the transferred interest (as it is gifted to the donee) is increased by the amount of such losses

4.) An exchange of a taxpayer's interest in a passive activity in a nontaxable transaction (such as a like-kind exchange) does not trigger suspended losses

a.) The gain is treated as passive income against which passive losses may be deducted to the extent that any boot (taxable gain) is received in such transaction

> **EXAMPLE (At-Risk Rules and Passive Activity Loss Rules)** Reggie is a high-income wage earner currently earning $180,000 annually. Recently, he has invested $30,000 for a 15% interest in a RELP as a limited partner. Operations of the activity resulted in a loss of $300,000, of which Reggie's share is $45,000. Reggie does not have any passive income in the current year. As a result, $15,000 of Reggie's loss is suspended under the at-risk rules, which leaves a potential remaining deduction of $30,000. This $30,000 loss is suspended under the passive activity loss rules because Reggie does not have any passive income with which to offset the income, and he has not disposed of his entire interest in the passive activity in the current year.

b. Suspended losses unused at the time of the investor-taxpayer's death are deductible on the taxpayer's final tax return subject to two rules:

1.) If the basis of the investment in the passive activity receives a step up to fair market value (FMV) in the decedent-investor's estate, the suspended losses are reduced by the amount of the increase to FMV

2.) If the basis of the investment receives a step down to fair market value (FMV) in the decedent-investor's estate, then the full amount of suspended losses in the activity is deductible on the decedent's final income tax return

> **EXAMPLE (Suspended Losses at Death)** Mavis died owning an investment in a passive activity for which she had a basis of $50,000. The fair market value of her investment in the activity was $70,000. She had suspended losses in the activity of $40,000. The deduction for the suspended losses on Mavis's final Form 1040 would be $20,000, or the excess of FMV over her basis. If Mavis's investment in the passive activity has instead received a step down to a fair market value of $30,000, the entire $40,000 in suspended losses would be deductible on her final Form 1040.

XIV. EMPLOYEE EXPENSES

A. TYPE OF DEDUCTION

1. Employees who incur certain expenses while performing their job duties are allowed a deduction for these amounts
2. Most unreimbursed employee expenses are miscellaneous itemized deductions subject to the 2% of AGI floor
   a. Exceptions
      1.) Impairment-related work expenses of handicapped individuals are miscellaneous itemized deductions not subject to the 2% floor
      2.) Moving expenses are a deduction for AGI (above-the-line)
3. For a self-employed taxpayer, job-related expenses are deductions for AGI (typically reported on Schedule C)

B. TRANSPORTATION

1. Expenditures allowed
   a. Unreimbursed expenditures related to transportation from one place to another while on company business are deductions from AGI (miscellaneous itemized deductions subject to the 2% of AGI floor)
   b. Employee cannot be in travel status
   c. Examples are automobile expenses, parking, and taxi fares
2. Commuting
   a. Normally disallowed (personal expense)
   b. Exceptions that allow a deduction
      1.) Transporting heavy tools (incremental cost only)
      2.) A commute to a second job (based on distance between jobs; location of taxpayer home is irrelevant)
      3.) Employer requires employee to travel between work stations (expenses between work stations only are deductible)
      4.) Taxpayer commutes to a temporary work location (generally defined as less than one year)

EXHIBIT 16: When Are Transportation Expenses Deductible?

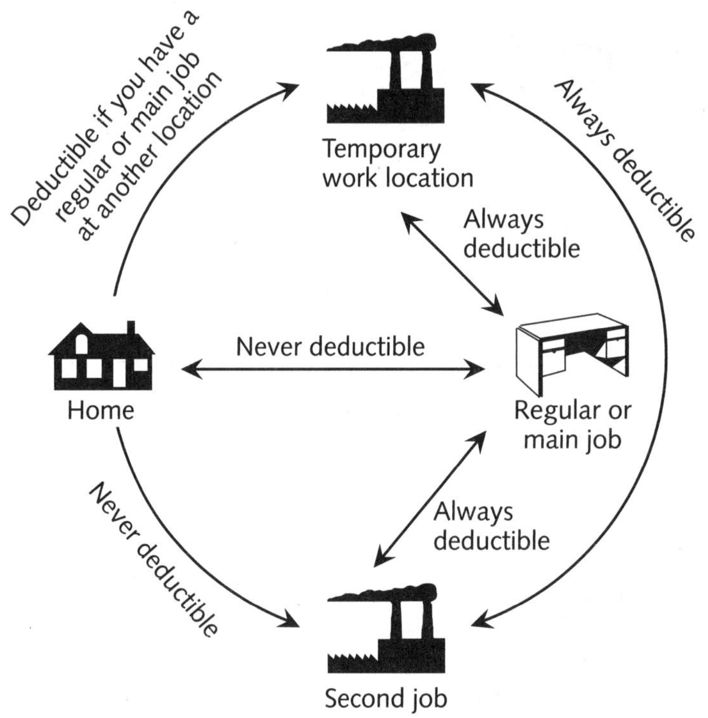

Home: The place where you reside. Transportation expenses between your home and your main or regular place of work are personal commuting expenses.

Regular or main job: Your principal place of business. If you have more than one job, you must determine which one is your regular or main job. Consider the time you spend at each, the activity you have at each, and the income you earn at each.

Temporary work location: A place where your work assignment is realistically expected to last (and does in fact last) one year or less. Unless you have a regular place of business, you can only deduct transportation expenses to a temporary work location outside your metropolitan area.

Second job: If you regularly work at two or more places in one day, whether or not for the same employer, you can deduct your transportation expenses of getting from one workplace to another. If you do not go directly from your first job to your second job, you can only deduct the transportation expenses of going directly from your first job to your second job. You cannot deduct your transportation expenses between your home and a second job on a day off from your main job.

IRS Publication 17; Figure 26-B

3. Calculation of auto expenses
   a. Actual operating cost method
      1.) Examples include depreciation, gas, licenses, maintenance, and insurance
      2.) Must be prorated between business and personal use
   b. Automatic mileage method—a fixed dollar amount of money per business mile plus tolls and parking
   c. General rules—either method is acceptable, with the following constraints
      1.) Vehicle must be owned or leased by the taxpayer claiming the deduction
      2.) Only one vehicle can be used at a given time
      3.) If standard mileage rate is used in year 1, MACRS cannot be used later
      4.) If election to expense under Section 179 or MACRS is used in year 1, no change to the automatic mileage method is allowed

C. TRAVEL

1. Must be away from tax home
   a. To deduct travel expenses, the taxpayer must determine the location of the tax home
   b. Generally, the taxpayer's tax home is the regular place of business or post of duty regardless of where the taxpayer maintains the family home
   c. If the taxpayer does not maintain a residence or have a regular place of business, the taxpayer is considered a transient (an itinerant)
      1.) The tax home is wherever the taxpayer is currently working
      2.) As a transient, the taxpayer cannot claim a travel expense deduction because the taxpayer is never considered away from home

> **EXAMPLE** Tiffany lives in Cincinnati where she has a seasonal job for eight months and earns $90,000. She works the remaining four months in Miami, also at a seasonal job, and earns $30,000. Therefore, Cincinnati is her main place of work because she spends most of her time and earns most of her income in that city.

2. Description of deduction
   a. Transportation, meals, lodging, and incidentals while away from home on business
   b. Expenditures are unreimbursed expenses and are miscellaneous itemized deductions subject to the 2% of AGI floor
   c. An overnight stay is required. Overnight is defined as substantially longer than a work day.
   d. Meals and lodging are not deductible if the travel is a single-day trip. When allowable, meals are limited to a 50% deduction.

3. The employee's absence from home must be temporary in nature
    a. A temporary assignment must be one year or less. If assignment is more than one year, the tax home changes and the away-from-home requirement is not met.
    b. The taxpayer's household cannot be moved to the new location
4. Restrictions on certain types of business travel
    a. Conventions must be related to the trade or business to be classified as deductible travel
    b. Spousal travel is disallowed unless it is for a bona fide business purpose
    c. Deductions for travel on cruise ships are limited to twice the highest per diem amount allowed for a day of domestic travel by employees in the executive branch of the federal government
    d. While expenses associated with attending a meeting or seminar related to income-producing activities are not allowed, they are deductible if connected with the taxpayer's trade or business
5. Combined business and pleasure travel
    a. Domestic travel
        1.) A domestic trip must be primarily for business purposes in order to deduct transportation expenses
        2.) If primarily business, taxpayer can deduct 100% of transportation expenses
        3.) If not primarily business, taxpayer cannot deduct transportation expenses
        4.) Other expenses must be allocated between business and personal

> **EXAMPLE** Marlene works in Atlanta and takes a business trip to New Orleans. On her way home, she stops in Mobile to visit her parents. She spends $630 for the nine days she was away from home for travel, meals, lodging, and other travel expenses. If she had not stopped in Mobile, she would have been gone only six days and her total cost would have been $580. She can deduct $580 for her trip, including the cost of round-trip transportation to and from New Orleans. The cost of her meals is subject to the 50% limit on meal expenses.

    b. Foreign travel
        1.) An allocation of transportation expenses is required between business and personal travel unless:
            a.) the total time is seven days or less;
            b.) less than 25% of the time was spent on personal travel;
            c.) the taxpayer has no control over the schedule; or
            d.) the desire for vacation is not a major factor in deciding to take the trip

EXAMPLES

- Victor traveled to Paris primarily for business. He left Denver on Tuesday and flew to New York. On Wednesday, he flew from New York to Paris, arriving the next morning. On Thursday and Friday, he had business discussions, and from Saturday until Tuesday, he was sightseeing. He flew back to New York, arriving Wednesday afternoon. On Thursday, he flew back to Denver. Although Victor was away from his home in Denver for more than a week, he was not outside the United States for more than a week because the day of departure does not count as a day outside the United States. He can deduct his cost of the round-trip flight between Denver and Paris. He can also deduct the cost of his stay in Paris for Thursday and Friday while he conducted business. However, he cannot deduct the cost of his stay in Paris from Saturday through Tuesday because those days were spent on nonbusiness activities.
- Jody flew from Seattle to Tokyo. She spent 14 days on business and 5 days on personal matters and then flew back to Seattle. She spent one day flying in each direction. Because only 5 of the 21 days (less than 25%) of her total time abroad was for nonbusiness activities, she can deduct as travel expenses what it would have cost her to make the trip if she had not engaged in any nonbusiness activity. The amount she can deduct is the cost of the round-trip plane fare and 16 days (14 days plus the 2 days of travel) of meals (subject to the 50% limit), lodging, and other related expenses.

EXAMPLE Allison took a trip from Montgomery, Alabama, to London, England. She was away from home for 10 days. She spent two days vacationing and eight days on business (including the two travel days). Her expenses are as follows:

Airfare	$1,200
Lodging (10 days × $150)	$1,500
Meals (10 days × $90)	$900

Allison's deduction is $2,760 [$1,200 + (8 × $150) + ½ (8 × $90) = $2,760]. Less than 25% of the time was personal, so no allocation of transportation expenses is required.

EXHIBIT 17: Travel Expenses You Can Deduct

IF you have expenses for...	THEN you can deduct the cost of...
transportation	travel by airplane, train, bus, or car between your home and your business destination. If you were provided with a ticket or you are riding free as a result of a frequent traveler or similar program, your cost is zero. If you travel by ship, see *Luxury Water Travel* and *Cruise Ships* (under *Conventions*) for additional rules and limits.
taxi, commuter bus, and airport limousine	fares for these and other types of transportation that take you between: ■ The airport or station and your hotel, and ■ The hotel and the work location of your customers or clients, your business meeting place, or your temporary work location.
baggage and shipping	sending baggage and sample or display material between your regular and temporary work locations.
car	operating and maintaining your car when traveling away from home on business. You can deduct actual expenses or the standard mileage rate, as well as business-related tolls and parking. If you rent a car while away from home on business, you can deduct only the business-use portion of the expenses.
lodging and meals	your lodging and meals if your business trip is overnight or long enough that you need to stop for sleep or rest to properly perform your duties. Meals include amounts spent for food, beverages, taxes, and related tips. See *Meals* for additional rules and limits.
cleaning	dry cleaning and laundry.
telephone	business calls while on your business trip. This includes business communication by fax machine or other communication devices.
tips	tips you pay for any expenses in this chart.
other	other similar ordinary and necessary expenses related to your business travel. These expenses might include transportation to or from a business meal, public stenographer's fees, computer rental fees, and operating and maintaining a house trailer.

IRS Publication 463, Table 1-1

D. EDUCATION EXPENSES

1. General requirements for deductibility
    a. To maintain or improve existing skills in the present job—nondegree classes are allowed as long as they maintain or improve existing skills
    b. To meet legally imposed or employer requirements to retain current job, such as continuing education requirements

2. Nondeductible expenses
   a. To meet minimum requirements of the current job (education degree to become a teacher)
   b. To qualify the taxpayer for a new job (law degree)
   c. For review classes or exams such as the CPA or bar exam
3. Allowable expenditures
   a. Direct expenses
      1.) Books
      2.) Tuition
      3.) Typing and photocopying
   b. Indirect expenses
      1.) Transportation (i.e., from office to school)
      2.) Travel
         a.) Meals subject to 50% reduction
         b.) Lodging
      3.) Laundry while in travel status

EXAMPLE Dawn, who holds a bachelor's degree in art history, is a middle school teacher in New Orleans. She wants to further her education in art history, believing this will allow her to become a better teacher. Dawn spent her summer break attending the University of Hawaii taking art history courses. Her expenses are as follows:

Books and tuition	$2,000
Meals	1,000
Lodging	700
Laundry while in travel status	200
Transportation	700
Total	$4,600

What is Dawn's education expense deduction?

Answer: $4,100 [$2,000 + .5 ($1,000) + ($700 + $200 + $700) = $4,100]. The shortcut would be to take the total and deduct 50% of the meals. Before taking this approach, it would be wise to check each category and make sure it is actually deductible.

EXHIBIT 18: Deductible Educational Expenses Flow Diagram

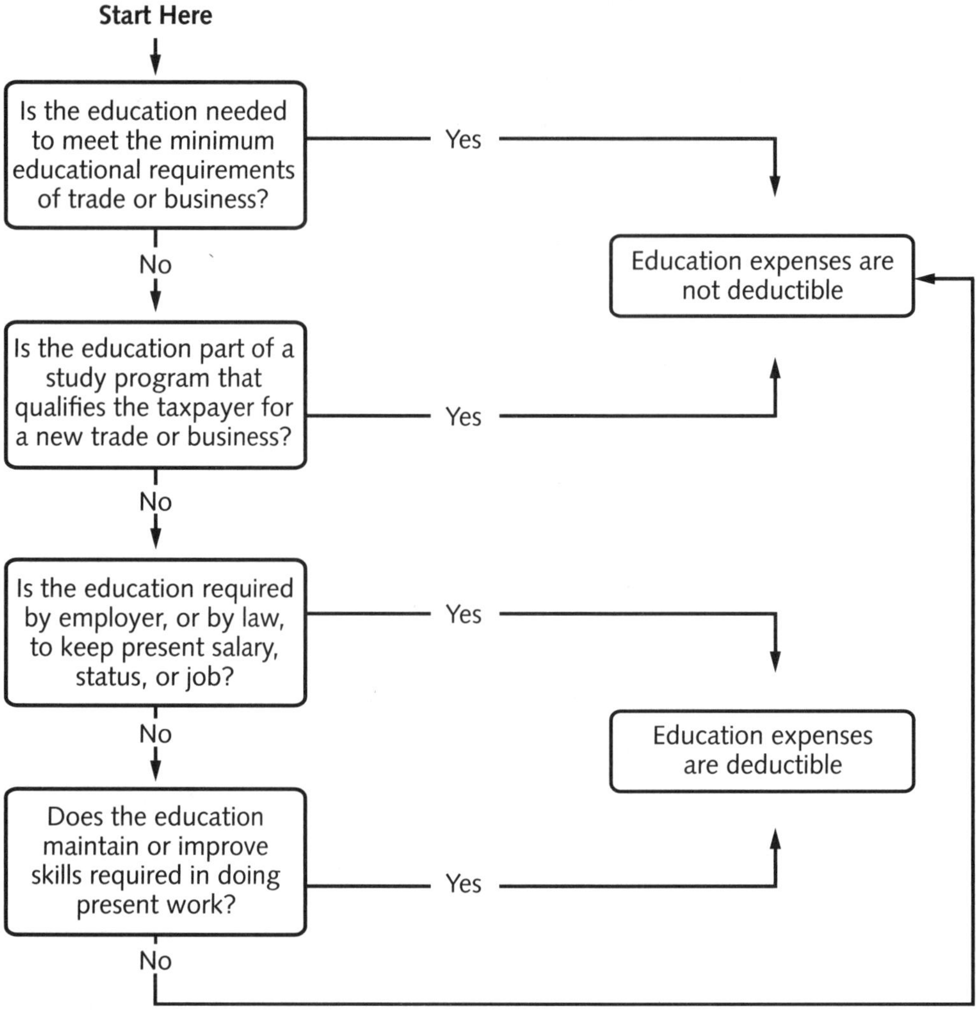

IRS Publication 17

E. MEALS AND ENTERTAINMENT (ONLY 50% DEDUCTIBLE)

1. Meals and entertainment expenses are subject to the 50% reduction
   a. Meals—including taxes and tips
   b. Entertainment—including cover charges, parking, and entertainment room rentals
2. Exceptions—these are 100% deductible
   a. Transportation (e.g., cab fare)
   b. If the full value of expenditure is included in employee's compensation
   c. If the value is de minimis
   d. If it is a company event (e.g., parties or picnics)

3. Classification of expenses
   a. Directly related to business
      1.) Entertainment precedes or follows an actual business meeting
      2.) Not necessary for actual benefit to occur but must have expectation of benefit
      3.) The expenditure should be in a clear business setting
   b. Associated with business
      1.) Promoting goodwill and maintaining customer relations
      2.) Must intend to obtain new business or to continue existing business
   c. Substantiation
      1.) Amount
      2.) Date and duration
      3.) Place
      4.) Business purpose
      5.) Names and business relationships of the parties involved
      6.) The previous information is generally easily attainable from receipts and notations on the affected receipts of the additional information needed
4. Restrictions
   a. Business meals
      1.) Directly related to or associated with a business meeting
      2.) Must be reasonable cost
      3.) Taxpayer must be present at the meal
   b. Club dues
      1.) No deduction allowed
      2.) Entertainment costs while at club may still qualify (subject to 50% deductibility)
   c. Tickets for entertainment
      1.) Eligible amount is limited to face value of the tickets plus tax (but not fees)
      2.) Skybox amount limited to number of seats available (even if all are not used) multiplied by price of regular seats
      3.) Subject to 50% deductibility
   d. Business gifts
      1.) Limited to $25 per donee per year
      2.) Gifts less than $4 and promotional items (e.g., pens with business name) are excluded from limits
      3.) Additional deductions allowed for incidental costs (e.g., engraving, delivery, gift wrapping)

4.) No deduction allowed for gifts to superiors or employers

5.) Employee achievement nonqualified plan awards based on length of service or safety under $400 are excluded

e. Unreimbursed entertainment expenses of employees

1.) Subject to the 2% of AGI floor for unreimbursed business expenses

2.) The 50% reduction on meal and entertainment expenses is applied before combining the expenses with any other miscellaneous itemized deductions of the taxpayer and applying the 2% of AGI floor

EXAMPLES

- Kay entertains one of her clients and incurs the following:

Taxi	$30
Door cover fee	25
Dinner	128
Tips to waitress	25
Total	$208

Assuming proper substantiation, Kay's deduction is $119 calculated as follows: $30 + 50%($25 + $128 + $25) = $119.

- Chelsea, the sales director for a software company, pays $2,000 to obtain a skybox for an evening production of *Cats*. The skybox holds 15 seats, and Chelsea invites 14 clients. Nonluxury seats sell for $25 each. The refreshments served to Chelsea and her clients cost $455. A substantial business discussion was held before and after the show, and Chelsea has all necessary substantiation. Chelsea's deduction is $415: 50%[(15 seats × $25) + $455] = $415.

- Elizabeth made the following gifts during the current year:

To Candace, a key client ($4 of the amount listed was for gift wrapping)	$104
To Kathy, Elizabeth's secretary, on Kathy's birthday	24
To Jan, Elizabeth's boss, at Christmas	28
Total gifts	$156

Assuming proper substantiation, Elizabeth's deduction is $53 [$29 ($25 + $4) + $24 = $53]. The cost of gift wrapping is allowed. No deduction is available for a gift to a superior. The $25 in the equation is the $25 per person limit.

F. HOME OFFICE

1. Taxpayers may deduct expenses attributable to a home office used in a business if the home office qualifies under one or more of the following tests:

a. Principal place of business

1.) A home office will be considered a principal place of business if it is used exclusively and regularly by the taxpayer for administrative or management activities of a trade or business and there is no other fixed location where these activities are performed to a substantial extent

b. Used exclusively and regularly as a place of business used to meet clients or patients in the normal course of the trade or business

c. If it is a separate structure that is not attached to the dwelling, it must be used in connection with the trade or business

2. Deductions and limits

   a. Requires allocation of total household expenses

   b. Cannot exceed net income of business (i.e., cannot create a loss)

   c. Must first deduct expenses that would be normally allowed (i.e., taxes, mortgage interest)

   d. For self-employed individuals, the deduction is for AGI

   e. For employees, the deduction is from AGI (2% miscellaneous itemized deduction)

   f. Disallowed expenses can be carried forward

3. Coordination with personal residence gain exclusion

   a. When an individual taxpayer sells a principal residence, he can exclude up to $250,000 of gain ($500,000 if married) if he owns the home and uses it as a principal residence for at least two out of five years preceding the sale

   b. When a personal residence is also used for business purposes, such as a home office, and the home office use is in a separate structure from the personal residence (dwelling unit), the home must be divided into two properties when sold

      1.) The portion of the gain attributable to the personal use is generally eligible for the gain exclusion if it satisfies all of the Section 121 rules

      2.) The portion of the gain attributable to the business use may be taxable as a sale of a business asset

      3.) Taxpayer's basis in the residential property must be allocated between the personal use of the residence and the business use of the separate structure in the same proportions as the gain

      4.) Depreciation recovery must follow the rules for Section 1250 on the sale of real estate used in business

   c. If the home office portion was not a separate structure from the dwelling unit and the principal residence satisfies the requirements of Section 121 for the gain exclusion

      1.) The taxpayer can exclude the gain on the entire residence

      2.) Gain attributable to depreciation deductions occurring after May 6, 1997, will still be taxable

EXAMPLE Jerry, an unmarried individual, purchased a residence on May 1, 2004. He originally used the entire home as a personal residence. On June 1, 2008, he began using 15% of the home as a home office. He continued to use the home office until May 1, 2010, when he sold the home.

Because he used his entire home as a personal residence for 25 months during the five-year period before the sale, he will qualify for the maximum exclusion of up to $250,000 on the gain attributable to the residential portion of the property sale. However, any gain attributable to depreciation claimed will be taxable to Jerry.

If, instead, the home office were located in a separate building on the property, Jerry would have to allocate 15% of the basis and 15% of the gain to the home office as though they were two separate properties. The depreciation taken would be recaptured as taxable gain on the home office portion of the property sale and the 15%home office portion of the property treated as a sale of a business asset. The $250,000 gain exclusion would only apply to the residential portion of the property sale.

G. JOB HUNTING EXPENSES

1. Seeking new employment in the same trade or business is deductible whether or not the taxpayer gets the job
2. Seeking employment in different trade or business is not deductible under any circumstances
3. Deductible expenses include travel, printing, postage, and employment agency fees
4. No deduction is allowed if you are seeking employment for the first time

H. OTHER EMPLOYEE EXPENSES

1. Classified as miscellaneous itemized deductions, subject to the 2% of AGI floor
   a. Professional dues and subscriptions
   b. Union dues and work uniforms
   c. Malpractice insurance premiums
2. Miscellaneous expenses not subject to 2% floor
   a. Impairment-related work expenses of handicapped individuals
   b. Gambling losses to the extent of gambling winnings

I. REIMBURSED EMPLOYEE EXPENSES

1. Accountable plans
   a. Requires adequate accounting of all expenditures
   b. Employee must return any unused allowance

3. What is not covered
   a. Unnecessary cosmetic surgery
   b. Funerals
4. Diagnosis, cure, mitigation, treatment, or prevention of disease
   a. Examples: hospital charges, doctor's fees, glasses, insurance premiums, stop-smoking programs, surgery to correct vision, legal abortion, and weight loss programs
   b. Prescription medicines and insulin
   c. Nursing home expenditures (including meals) may be allowed if medical care is primary reason for admittance
   d. Cost of lead-based paint removal
   e. Surgery to correct a congenital deformity or disfiguring disease
   f. Tuition for a special school may be allowed if the school has special facilities or if medical care related to the infirmity is received
   g. Capital expenditures—allowable with some restrictions
      1.) Expenditures are of a medical nature
      2.) Expenditures are on the advice of a physician
      3.) Facilities are used primarily by patient alone
      4.) Facilities are built at a reasonable expense
      5.) Operating and maintenance expenditures are also allowable
      6.) Appraisal costs for determining the change in value are also allowable (miscellaneous itemized deduction subject to 2% of AGI floor)
      7.) Limited to the amount by which the expenditures exceed any increase in the value of the property
      8.) Deduction is only allowed while the medical condition exists
      9.) The 7.5% of AGI floor applies to capital expenditures
5. Transportation and lodging
   a. These expenditures are allowed as medical expenses (subject to 7.5% of AGI floor)
   b. Examples include fares, ambulance, personal car, tolls, and parking. Personal car allowance can be actual expenses or standard rate.
   c. Includes the travel costs of a parent with a minor child
   d. Includes the travel costs of any person who must travel with the patient
   e. Lodging is included, with some restrictions
      1.) Must be primarily and essentially for medical care
      2.) The medical care must be in a licensed medical care facility
      3.) Accommodations must be reasonable
      4.) No significant element of personal pleasure can be involved
      5.) Limited to $50 per night for each person

f. No meal deduction is allowed, with one exception
   1.) If meals are provided on site and are part of the medical care
   2.) The 50% meal deductibility does not apply to this exception

6. Qualified long-term care expenses
   a. Medical services for a chronically ill person that are provided under a prescribed plan of care
      1.) Chronically ill is defined as being unable to perform (without substantial assistance from another individual) at least two activities of daily living (e.g., eating, dressing, bathing) for a period of at least 90 days because of a loss of functional capacity
   b. Includes expenditures for diagnostic, therapeutic, preventive, rehabilitative, and personal care services

7. Health insurance premiums
   a. Expenditures for accident and health insurance premiums are deductible (subject to 7.5% of AGI floor)
      1.) Individual and group policies are covered
      2.) Any premiums paid by the employer are not deductible by the employee
      3.) Special rules for self-employed persons
         a.) 100% of the health insurance premiums can be deducted for AGI
         b.) No deduction is allowed for premiums paid by an employee if an employer-paid plan is available
   b. The premiums paid for long-term care are qualifying medical expenses subject to the 7.5% of AGI floor. The maximum deductible premium depends on the taxpayer's age.

EXHIBIT 19: 2011 Maximum Deductible Long-Term Care Premiums (Subject to 7.5% of AGI Floor)

Attained Age Before Close of Taxable Year	Annual Maximum Deductible Premiums
40 or less	$340
More than 40 but not more than 50	$640
More than 50 but not more than 60	$1,270
More than 60 but not more than 70	$3,390
More than 70	$4,240

8. Year of deduction
   a. A deduction is available in the year paid for both cash-basis and accrual-basis taxpayers
   b. A deduction is available in the year incurred for deceased taxpayers
   c. If a payment is made on a credit card, the payment is deemed to have been made at the time of the charge

d. A current deduction is not allowed for prepayment of future medical care unless the taxpayer is under a^ obligation to make the payment

9. Reimbursements

a. Expected reimbursen. ; are disregarded in determining the amount of deduction

b. Tax benefit rule applies ʻmbursement occurs in a future year

c. Reimbursement is conside rt of gross income if a tax benefit resulted

> **EXAMPLE** Mae, an er. ɾe of XYZ Company, has an AGI of $20,000. She incurred the following medical e ᵓs (she itemizes her deductions):
>
> | | |
> |---|---|
> | Health insurance premiums | $8: |
> | Dental expenses | $500 |
> | Unreimbursed medical | $450 ($:dical expenses – $550 reimbursement) |
>
> Her total medical expenses are $1,800 \ $500 + $450). She must reduce this amount by 7.5% of her AGI. Mae's deductibl. :al expenses are $300: [$1,800 – $1,500 or (7.5% of $20,000)].

C. TAXES

1. Summary of deductible taxes

a. State, local, and foreign real property taxes

b. State and local personal property taxes (if tax is based on va ɾf property)

c. State, local, and foreign income taxes

d. State and local sales taxes that could be deducted in lieu of dedu. for state and local income taxes expired December 31, 2009

2. Real estate taxes, assessments, and apportionment of taxes

a. Real estate taxes

1.) Deductible as an itemized deduction for the person the taxes are imp. on regardless of who pays them

2.) Must be based on the value of the property (ad valorem)

b. Assessments

1.) Imposed for purposes of local benefit (e.g., roads, schools), actions that typical. increase the value of the property

2.) Usually not deductible but added to the basis of the property

c. Apportionment for real estate transfers

1.) Based on the number of days each held the property during the tax year

a.) Day of sale goes to the buyer

2.) Apportionment rules govern the deduction, not the purchase agreement

3.) Based on the date of the transfer

4.) If purchase agreement does not apportion, basis adjustment is required

a.) If buyer pays all the tax

- Seller's portion is added to the amount realized by the seller
- Buyer's basis is increased by the same amount

b.) If seller pays all the tax

- Buyer's portion is deducted from the amount realized by the seller
- Buyer's basis is reduced by the same amount

3. State and local income taxes
   a. These taxes paid are deductible as itemized deductions only
   b. For cash-basis taxpayers, the amount included is the withheld amount
   c. State and local estimated tax payments are also allowed as deductions
   d. Refunds occurring in future years are included in gross income at that time, to the extent a tax benefit was received
   e. Any state income taxes that are paid, whether for the previous, current, or future year, are deducted in the year paid
4. Real estate taxes and state/local income taxes incurred in a trade or business or on production of income property are deductions for AGI
5. State and local general sales taxes (expired December 31, 2009)
   a. Individual taxpayers may elect to deduct either state and local income taxes or state and local sales taxes as an itemized deduction
      1.) Individuals should consider whether to make this election, depending on their relative amounts of state and local income taxes compared to sales taxes
      2.) This election would especially be appropriate for taxpayers residing in a state that does not impose a state income tax
   b. Amount of deduction
      1.) The taxpayer can deduct the actual amount of general sales taxes paid. This would require the taxpayer to accumulate receipts showing sales taxes paid.
      2.) Alternatively, the taxpayer may determine his deduction using standardized IRS tables. If the standard IRS tables are used, the taxpayer can claim an additional deduction for sales taxes paid for the purchase of a motor vehicle or boat.

D. INTEREST

1. Investment interest
   a. Interest on funds borrowed to acquire investment assets
   b. Deduction for investment interest is limited to net taxable investment income
      1.) Investment income
         a.) Examples include gross income from interest, dividends, annuities, and royalties
         b.) Qualified dividends (taxed at the reduced rates) are not included in investment income
         c.) Capital gains, taxed at the capital gain rate, are not included in investment income
         d.) Cannot be derived in the ordinary course of business
         e.) Does not include tax-exempt interest income
      2.) Investment expenses
         a.) Must be directly connected with the production of income
         b.) Do not include interest expense in investment expenses for this calculation
         c.) Examples include subscriptions to professional newsletters, safe deposit box rentals, portfolio management fees
         d.) Does not include commissions incurred in buying or selling investments
   c. Net investment income equals gross investment income less deductible investment expenses (other than investment interest) in excess of 2% of AGI
   d. Carryover of disallowed investment interest allowed indefinitely

EXAMPLE Mario had the following items of income and expense for the current year:

Interest income from Carall Company bonds	$5,000
Interest income from State of Louisiana bonds	$1,000
Margin interest expense (investment interest expense)	($7,000)

If he itemizes, Mario can only deduct $5,000 of the investment interest expense (subject to the 2% AGI floor). His taxable investment income is $5,000 ($5,000 taxable interest). The State of Louisiana bonds are municipal bonds; therefore, the interest is tax exempt.

2. Qualified residence interest
   a. Interest paid or incurred on debt for the purchase of a qualified residence of the taxpayer is deductible
      1.) Qualified residence includes a primary residence and one other residence
      2.) May include a condo, trailer, boat with living quarters, and mobile homes
      3.) The debt must be secured by the property
      4.) Maximum allowable acquisition indebtedness is $1 million ($500,000 for married filing separately)
      5.) Acquisition indebtedness also includes construction and substantial improvements
   b. Home equity loans are also covered. Interest is deductible on the indebtedness to the lesser of:
      1.) Fair market value (FMV) less acquisition indebtedness; or
      2.) $100,000
   c. Interest on home equity loans not used for home improvements is not considered qualified residence interest for the purposes of the alternative minimum tax (AMT) and is added back for the calculation of AMTI

> **EXAMPLE** Rose and Mark are married and own a home with a fair market value (FMV) of $425,000. The current balance on the first mortgage is $330,000. If the couple takes out a home equity loan in the amount of $100,000, how much of the interest on the debt will be treated as qualified residence interest if the home subsequently decreases in value by $25,000? Subsequent devaluation of the home does not require that the deductibility of the home equity loan interest be re-evaluated. The calculation is made using the FMV and subtracting the outstanding home acquisition debt for each home on the date that the last debt was secured by the home. Interest on $95,000 of the loan is deductible ($425,000 FMV – $330,000 first mortgage balance).

3. Interest paid as points
   a. Points on a home loan are deductible in the year paid (principal residence loans only)
      1.) Borrower (buyer) is treated as paying any points seller paid for borrower's mortgage
      2.) Can deduct points up to funds provided plus seller-paid points
      3.) Buyer must reduce basis in home by points paid by seller. Seller reduces amount realized by this amount.
   b. Points on refinancing must be capitalized and amortized over the life of the loan. However, if refinancing is incurred for home improvements and the points are paid from separate funds, the points are currently deductible.

> **EXAMPLE**
>
> - When Gary took out a $100,000 mortgage loan to buy his home in the current year, he was charged one percentage point ($1,000). He met all the tests for deducting points, except the only funds he provided were a $750 down payment. Of the $1,000 charged for points, he can deduct $750 in the current year.
> - When Stephanie took out a $100,000 mortgage loan to buy her home in the current year, she was charged one percentage point ($1,000). Tim, who sold her the home, also paid one point ($1,000) to help her get her mortgage. Stephanie met all the tests for deducting points, except the only funds she provided were a $750 down payment. In the current year, Stephanie can deduct $1,750 ($750 of the amount she was charged plus the $1,000 paid by Tim). She must reduce the basis of her home by the $1,000 paid by Tim.

4. Prepayment penalty—considered to be interest paid and is deductible (if the interest itself is eligible)
5. Interest paid to related parties
   a. Deductible according to normal interest rules
   b. Refer to rules on loans to related parties
6. Other restrictions
   a. Cannot deduct interest paid on behalf of another (e.g., child, parent)
   b. Prepaid interest deduction is based on accrual-basis rules for all taxpayers
7. Classification
   a. If interest is paid for a business use or the production of income, it is deductible for AGI
   b. If interest is paid for personal use (investment interest and qualified residence interest), it is deductible from AGI
8. Personal interest (also sometimes called consumer interest) is not deductible (e.g., credit cards, personal auto loans)

> **EXAMPLE** During the current year, Albert paid the following interest charges:
>
> | | |
> |---|---|
> | Home mortgage | $9,000 |
> | On loan to purchase household furniture (personal) | $800 |
> | On loan to purchase State of Louisiana general obligation bonds (tax exempt) | $750 |
>
> If Albert itemizes his deductions for the current year, the amount deductible as interest expense is $9,000. The interest on the loan to purchase household furniture is nondeductible consumer interest. The interest on the loan to purchase State of Louisiana bonds is not deductible.

9. Certain taxpayers may deduct interest paid on a higher education loan. See Section VI (L) Interest on Educational Loans.

E. CHARITABLE CONTRIBUTIONS

1. Must be made to a qualified organization

   a. Types of organizations for which donations qualify for a charitable deduction

      1.) US District of Columbia, a state or possession of the United States, or a political subdivision of a state or possession

      2.) Organizations located in the United States that are organized and operated exclusively for religious, charitable, scientific, literary, or educational purposes or for the prevention of cruelty to children or animals

      3.) Veterans' organizations

      4.) Cemetery companies

      5.) IRS Publication 78 lists qualified charitable organizations. This information can also be obtained from **www.irs.gov**.

EXHIBIT 21: Examples of Charitable Contributions—A Quick Check

Use the following lists for a quick check of contributions you can or cannot deduct. See Publication 17; Section 24 for more information and additional rules and limits that may apply.

Deductible as Charitable Contributions	Not Deductible as Charitable Contributions
■ Money or property you give to — Churches, synagogues, temples, mosques, and other religious organizations — Federal, state, and local governments, if your contribution is solely for public purposes (e.g., a gift to reduce the public debt) — Nonprofit schools and hospitals — Public parks and recreation facilities — Salvation Army, Red Cross, CARE, Goodwill Industries, United Way, Boy Scouts, Girl Scouts, Boys and Girls Clubs of America, and etc. — War veterans' groups ■ Costs you pay for a student living with you, sponsored by a qualified organization ■ Out-of-pocket expenses when you serve a qualified organization as a volunteer	■ Money or property you give to: — Civic leagues, social sports clubs, labor unions, and chambers of commerce — Foreign organizations (except certain Canadian, Israeli, and Mexican charities) — Groups that are run for personal profit — Groups whose purpose is to lobby for law changes — Homeowners' associations — Individuals — Political groups or candidates for public office ■ Cost of raffle, bingo, or lottery tickets ■ Dues, fees, or bills paid to country clubs, lodges, fraternal orders, or similar groups ■ Tuition ■ Value of your time or services ■ Value of blood given to a blood bank

IRS Publication 17; Table 24-1

2. Qualifying organizations are also classified as the following:
   a. Public charities
      1.) Receive broad public support
      2.) General examples—churches, educational institutions, hospitals, medical research organizations
      3.) Specific examples—American Red Cross, Girl Scouts, United Way, Goodwill, Mercer University
   b. Private foundations
      1.) Not defined directly in the Code but rather by reference to a list of the types of organizations that are not private foundations
      2.) Typically funded by large contributions from a small number of contributors and income from investments and businesses unrelated to the foundation's charitable purposes
      3.) Usually function as charities by making grants to organizations that conduct charitable activities, instead of performing the activities themselves
3. Deduction is allowed in year paid for both cash and accrual-basis taxpayers

4. Consequences of a benefit received by donor
   a. If benefit is inconsequential, may deduct in full
   b. If a consequential benefit is received, the contribution deduction must be reduced by the fair market value of the benefit
   c. The mere right to use property is considered neither cash nor other property and is not deductible
   d. There is a special rule for contributions related to the right to buy athletic tickets from universities—80% of donation qualifies as deductible charitable contribution
5. No deductions allowed for volunteering of services, but related personal expenses are deductible
   a. Mileage for charitable use of an automobile is based on a standard rate or actual unreimbursed expenses for oil and gas
   b. Rental value of property donated to and used by a qualified charity is not deductible
   c. Cost of child care while performing charity-related activities is nondeductible
   d. Donating blood is considered to be a nondeductible personal service
6. Recordkeeping
   a. Donor must have a canceled check, bank record, or a receipt from the donee organization
      1.) Must list amount of cash or description of property
         a.) Must list name of organization, date of contribution, and amount
         b.) Taxpayer must have receipt by due date of return or when return is filed
   b. Noncash property over $500 and less than or equal to $5,000
      1.) An appraisal is not required. However, taxpayers may wish to get an independent appraisal to support the deduction claimed.
   c. Noncash property over $5,000 ($10,000 for nonpublic stock)
      1.) Noncash contributions with a value over $5,000 must be substantiated by a qualified appraisal of the property. A summary of the appraisal must be attached to the donor's income tax return for the year in which the deduction is first claimed.
      2.) The appraisal requirement will also apply if a taxpayer donates, to one or more charities, a number of similar items (such as coins) with a total value exceeding $5,000
      3.) An appraisal is not required for contributions of publicly traded securities for which market quotes are readily available on an established securities market
      4.) The costs of an appraisal are not deductible as a charitable contribution. However, these costs are deductible by individuals as miscellaneous itemized deductions, subject to the 2% of AGI floor.

> **EXAMPLE** Gina graduated from Mumford University. She donated $2,000 to the athletic department of the university to guarantee priority to purchase two premium season tickets to home football games. In addition, Gina purchased two season tickets for the regular price of $500 ($250 each). Gina's charitable contribution for the current year is $1,600. Eighty percent of $2,000 is deductible because Gina is paying for the right to purchase tickets. The $500 expenditure for the tickets cannot be claimed because they provided Gina with a benefit.

8. Bargain sale to charity

   a. In general

      1.) A bargain sale to charity occurs when a donor or seller transfers property to a charity (or other tax-exempt organization) in exchange fc a sum that is less than the FMV of the property

      2.) Considered part sale and part charitable contribution allocated on a pro rata basis

   b. Income tax ramifications

      1.) The difference between the sales price of the a et and the seller's basis allocated to the asset will be a capital gain to the eller for income tax purposes

      2.) The difference between the FMV of the as t and the consideration received is considered the allowable amount of char ible contribution. The basis not allocated to the sale of the asset is the basis or the consideration of the charitable contribution.

   c. Basis allocation

      1.) The basis of the property sold i argain sale to charity must be allocated between the portion of the pr ty sold and the portion donated to charity

      2.) The formula to calculate the sis of the property sold is as follows:

$$\left(\frac{\text{Amount realized on sal} \quad \text{charity}}{\text{Fair market value of e} \quad \text{e property}}\right) \times \text{adjusted basis of entire property}$$

   d. Relationship to transfer r ules

      1.) Gift of a remaind iterest

         a.) A lifetim nsfer to charity is a gift of a partial interest

         b.) If a ch s interest in the transfer of property is a remainder interest (i.e. charity receives what remains after a noncharitable income benefi usually the donor, has received income for a specified time), strict r pply

         c.) ansfer in trust will qualify only if it is a charitable annuity trust, itrust, or a pooled income fund (See *Volume 6—Estate Planning* for iles for establishing charitable trusts)

         Taxpayer may obtain both an income tax and transfer tax (gift tax) deduction e.) The income tax deduction for a partial interest transfer is restricted to the percentage of AGI limitations, but the transfer (gift) tax deduction is unlimited so long as the transfer is made to a qualifying charitable organization

EXAMPLE Steve owns property with a basis of $60,000 and a current value of $120,000, which he sells to charity for $100,000. Steve must first allocate basis between the sale and the charitable gift.

Basis for property sold = ($100,000 ÷ 120,000) × $60,000 = $50,000

Therefore, Steve will have a capital gain of $50,000, calculated as follows:

Cash received from charity	$100,000
Less adjusted basis allocated to asset sale	(50,000)
Equals capital gain	$ 50,000

He will also have an FMV from the calculation of the charitable income tax deduction of $20,000, calculated as follows:

FMV of property transferred to charity	$120,000
Less sales price	(100,000)
Equals amount of the charitable contribution	$ 20,000

The adjusted tax basis for the calculation of the charitable income tax deduction is calculated as follows:

Total adjusted tax basis (ATB)	$60,000
Less allocated to sale	(50,000)
Equals ATB for charitable purposes	$10,000

EXAMPLE

- Clarence makes the following charitable donations:

	Basis	FMV
Inventory held for resale in Clarence's business (a sole proprietorship)	$ 8,000	$ 6,000
Stock in Roth Corp. held as an investment (acquired 2 years ago)	$10,000	$40,000
Coin collection held as an investment (acquired 10 years ago)	$ 1,000	$ 7,000

The inventory was given to a local public school. The Roth Corp. stock was given to Clarence's church and the coin collection was given to the Boy Scouts. Ignoring percentage limitations, Clarence's charitable contribution for the current year is $47,000.

Inventory is ordinary income property, but the FMV ($6,000) must be used if it is lower than the basis ($8,000). Stock is intangible property and is not subject to the tangible personal property use-related rules. A sale of the Roth Corp. stock would have yielded a long-term capital gain, so the full FMV qualified for the deduction ($40,000). The coin collection comes under the tangible personal property (unrelated use); therefore, the adjusted basis ($1,000) must be used ($6,000 + 40,000 + 1,000 = $47,000).

- Colleen, a calendar-year taxpayer, made the following charitable contributions:

	Basis	FMV
Cash to church	$ 5,000	$ 5,000
Unimproved land to the city of Violet, Louisiana	$40,000	$70,000

The land had been held as an investment and was acquired five years ago. Shortly after receipt, the city of Violet sold the land for $90,000. Colleen's AGI is $120,000. She has two options with respect to the contribution deduction. First, she can deduct the FMV of the land (limited to 30% of her AGI). In this case, the total deduction would be $41,000. Calculated as follows: $5,000 (cash) + $36,000 ($70,000 FMV, but limited to 30% of AGI, which is $120,000). The carryover for the next five years is $34,000 ($70,000 FMV – $36,000 current year deduction). Alternatively, she can deduct the adjusted basis, limited to 50% of AGI. The total deduction would be $40,000 for the land plus $5,000 cash, for a total of $45,000. There would be no carryover in this case.

e. Charitable contributions by business entities

1.) Partnerships and S corporations—as pass-through entities, the charitable contributions are deducted by the partners and shareholders on their individual income tax returns. The amount of the deduction is reported to the partners and S corporation shareholders on Schedule K-1.

2.) C corporations—the charitable deduction is reported on the corporation's income tax return (Form 1120). The deduction is based on the type of property donated, the type of organization to which the property is donated, and the corporation's taxable income before taking into account the charitable deduction.

a.) Ordinary income property (e.g., inventory)—generally, a corporation may deduct the basis of ordinary income property donated to charity

b.) Capital gain property—generally, the corporation may deduct the FMV of the capital gain property donated to charity. However, the deduction will be limited to the property's adjusted basis in the following situations:

- The property is tangible personal property that is use-unrelated. *Use-unrelated* means that the property is put to a use that is not related to the charity's exempt purpose.
- If it is *use-unrelated* property, the donor cannot elect to deduct FMV, subject to corporate income limitations
- If it is *use-related* property and the donor-taxpayer can choose to deduct the property's FMV, subject to corporate income limitations
- The property is donated to certain private foundations

c.) Limit on charitable deduction—the maximum charitable deduction a corporation can take in a taxable year is limited to 10% of the corporation's taxable income before certain deductions

- The deductions that are not taken into account include the charitable contribution deduction, the dividends-received deduction, net operating loss carryback, and capital loss carryback

> **EXAMPLE** In the current year, XYZ Corporation had net income from operations of $60,000 and received a dividend of $4,000 which is eligible for the 70% dividends-received deduction. During the year, the corporation donated $8,000 in cash to the University of New Jersey.
>
> The maximum charitable contribution deduction that XYZ is entitled to is $6,400 ($60,000 + $4,000 = $64,000 × 10% = $6,400).
>
> XYZ will have taxable income of $54,800 ($60,000 + $4,000 – $2,800 dividends-received deduction – $6,400 charitable-contribution deduction).

- Any disallowed deduction may be carried forward by the corporation for up to five years

> **EXAMPLE** Assume the same facts as the previous example. XYZ Corporation may carry forward the disallowed deduction of $1,600 ($8,000 donation – $6,400 deduction) for up to five years.

F. CASUALTY LOSSES FOR INDIVIDUALS

1. Section 165

a. Losses of nonbusiness property are limited to losses from fire, storm, shipwreck, or other casualty or theft

b. Casualties refer to losses meeting three criteria

1.) Identifiable event causing the loss

2.) Property damage results

3.) Event is sudden, unusual, and unexpected

> **EXAMPLES**
> - Car accident (unless willful negligence or willful act caused it)
> - Fires (unless taxpayers set it or paid someone else to)
> - Earthquake
> - Flood
> - Tornado
> - Vandalism

c. Cash or property received as compensation for or to repair or replace damaged property reduces the amount of the loss (i.e., insurance payment)

2. Events that are not casualties
   a. Termite damage
   b. Most drought-related losses are considered progressive deterioration and are not casualties
3. Theft losses
   a. Include larceny, embezzlement, and robbery but exclude misplaced items
   b. Theft losses are deducted in the year of discovery, not the year of theft. The deduction is only allowed to the extent that the loss exceeds the expected recovery from any insurance.
   c. If the insurance claim is greater than the adjusted basis, a gain is recognized
4. When to deduct casualty losses
   a. General rule—loss is deductible in the year the loss occurs (except theft losses). If a reasonable chance of recovery from insurance exists, no loss is allowed.
   b. Disaster area losses
      1.) When the President of the United States declares a disaster area, the losses may be deducted in the year preceding the actual loss
      2.) If previous year's taxes have already been filed, the taxpayer may file an amended return
5. Measuring the amount of loss
   a. Amount of loss
      1.) The amount of the loss is the lesser of:
         a.) the adjusted basis; or
         b.) decline in FMV resulting from the event
      2.) Losses from property held for partial business and partial personal use are determined separately for each portion

3.) Losses are reduced by any insurance recovery that would have been received, whether or not a claim was filed

4.) Appraisal or cost of repairs is generally required to determine the extent of the loss

b. The deduction for casualty losses on personal use property is reduced by both a $100 floor and by 10% of AGI. The $100 floor applies to each casualty event, but the 10% floor is applied to the aggregate casualty loss amount for the year.

c. Personal use property losses are itemized deductions

d. Certain disaster-related losses may have different rules created by Congress for that disaster. The taxpayer should consult a tax professional when calculating those casualty loss deductions.

EXAMPLE In 2011, Larry had art worth $10,000 (basis of $15,000) stolen from his apartment. During the year, he had a salary of $30,000 and no other deductions. Larry's itemized deduction from the theft of the art is $6,900.

Loss	$10,000	(lesser of basis or FMV)
Less 10% AGI (10% × $30,000)	(3,000)	
$100 floor	(100)	
Itemized deduction	$6,900	

G. MISCELLANEOUS ITEMIZED DEDUCTIONS

1. Deductions subject to 2% of AGI floor (some of these were discussed in the Employee Business Expense section)

a. Job search costs

1.) Deductible only if looking for job in present occupation

2.) Not necessary to get the job to get the tax deduction

3.) Includes employment agency fees, travel, resume expenses

b. Work clothes and uniforms

1.) Wearing must be a condition of employment

2.) Must not be suitable for everyday wear

3.) Full-time military uniforms are usually not deductible

c. Professional organization dues

d. Hobby expenses (to extent of hobby income)

e. Work tools if expected to last one year or less

f. Expenses to produce or collect income (e.g., safe deposit box used to store securities)

g. Expenses related to paying any tax (e.g., appraisal fees, tax preparation fees)

h. Other unreimbursed employee business expenses

2. Deductions not subject to 2% AGI floor
   a. Federal estate tax on income in respect of decedent (IRD)
   b. Gambling losses to extent of gambling winnings
   c. Unrecovered investment in annuity contract when annuity ceases because taxpayer died
   d. Impairment-related work expenses of handicapped taxpayer

H. OVERALL LIMITATION ON ITEMIZED DEDUCTIONS

1. When AGI exceeds $169,550 in 2011 ($84,775 for married filing separately), a taxpayer will begin to lose the benefit of some itemized deductions
   a. Reduction does not apply to medical expenses, investment interest, casualty losses, or gambling losses
   b. Adjustment is 3% of AGI above the threshold
   c. Maximum reduction is 80% of covered itemized deductions
   d. Reduction is made after other Code provisions (e.g., 2% AGI floor for miscellaneous items)
   e. This reduction takes effect with the sunset of EGTRRA

XVI. ALTERNATIVE MINIMUM TAX

A. GENERAL

1. This tax is a backup to the federal income tax to ensure that no taxpayer with substantial economic income can avoid significant tax liability by using deductions and exclusions
2. Applies to all taxpayers (individuals, trusts, estates, and corporations)
   a. Small corporations with average gross receipts over a three-tax-year period not exceeding $7.5 million are exempt
   b. Amount reduced to $5 million for the first three-tax-year period of existence

B. INDIVIDUAL ALTERNATIVE MINIMUM TAX

1. This tax parallels the regular federal income tax in many ways but uses adjustments and preferences to account for the differences. For example, both allow depreciation deductions, but the amount used in the calculation will be different.
2. The AMT is expected to continue to affect more middle income taxpayers each year if Congress does not permanently address the AMT rules

   NOTE: At the time of this printing, Congress has not enacted legislation to avoid the reestablishment of pre-2001 noninflation-adjusted AMT exemption amounts from taking effect in the 2011 tax year. Congress may take action to affect the exemption amount before the end of the tax year. Students are urged to understand the theory of alternative minimum taxation, rather than focus on the exemption amounts.

3. A taxpayer may have to pay the AMT in 2011 if his taxable income for regular tax purposes, combined with any adjustments and preference items, exceeds:
   a. $45,000 if married filing a joint return or a qualifying widower with dependent child;
   b. $33,750 if filing status is single or head of household; or
   c. $22,500 if filing status is married filing separately
   d. The exemptions are phased out at upper income levels
4. Calculating alternative minimum taxable income (AMTI):

	Regular taxable income
+	Positive AMT adjustments
–	Negative AMT adjustments
+	Tax preferences
=	AMTI

5. Then, to calculate alternative minimum tax (AMT):

	AMTI
–	AMT exemption
=	Minimum tax base
×	AMT rate
=	Tentative AMT
–	Regular income tax on taxable income
=	AMT

3.) A portion of the exclusion of gain on sale of certain small business stock (Section 1202)

a.) For Section 1202 qualified small business stock acquired after 9/27/10 and before 1/1/11, 100% of the gain on the sale of this stock is excluded from alternative minimum taxable income (Small Business Jobs Act of 2010)

4.) Accelerated depreciation in excess of straight-line depreciation on certain property placed in service before 1987

8. Exclusion items versus deferral items

a. The following AMT adjustments/preference items are considered exclusion items:

1.) Standard deduction

2.) Itemized deduction

3.) Personal exemption

4.) A portion of the exclusion of gain from qualified small business stock (Section 1202)

5.) Tax-exempt interest treated as a tax preference for AMT

6.) Percentage depletion treated as a tax preference for AMT

b. Any adjustment/preference item that is not an exclusion item is a deferral item and includes the following:

1.) Accelerated depreciation

2.) ISO bargain element

9. The exemption amount for 2011—different exemption amounts are used depending on the filing status of the taxpayer. The exemption is phased out across the board at a rate of $.25 for each dollar over the threshold amount.

Filing Status	Exemption Amount	Phaseout Threshold
Married, Joint	$45,000	$150,000
Single	$33,750	$112,500
Head of Household	$33,750	$112,500
Married, Separate	$22,500	$ 75,000

C. MINIMUM TAX CREDIT FOR INDIVIDUALS

1. In general

a. The alternative minimum tax paid in one year may be used as a credit against regular tax in a future year

b. The credit may be carried forward (not back) indefinitely

2. Exclusion versus deferral items
   a. For noncorporate taxpayers, the credit is only available to the extent the alternative minimum tax was attributable to deferral items, which are timing differences
      1.) The alternative minimum tax attributable to exclusion items is not available as a credit
   b. Determined by calculating the adjusted net minimum tax
      1.) The difference between the actual AMT paid and the AMT that would have been paid taking into account only exclusion items

EXAMPLE Dave, a single taxpayer, just filed his income tax return for 2011. With the return, Dave had to pay $35,000 of alternative minimum tax, resulting from the exercise of incentive stock options (deferral item) and some tax-exempt interest from private-activity bonds (exclusion item). If Dave had taken into account only the exclusion items (tax-exempt interest), his AMT liability would have only been $20,000. Therefore, his minimum tax credit is $15,000, calculated as follows:

AMT paid with return	$35,000
Less AMT based on exclusion items only	(20,000)
AMT based on deferral items (minimum tax credit)	$15,000

D. CORPORATE ALTERNATIVE MINIMUM TAX

1. Corporations may have to pay the AMT if taxable income for regular tax purposes, combined with any adjustments and preference items, exceeds $40,000. The exemption is phased out at a rate of $.25 for each dollar of AMTI in excess of $150,000.
2. Exemption from the AMT for small businesses
   a. Certain small businesses are exempt from the AMT
   b. In their first year of existence, all corporations are exempt
   c. In the second year of existence, the corporation would be exempt if its gross receipts were $5 million or less in the prior year
   d. In the third year (and going forward), the corporation would be exempt if its average annual gross receipts for all prior three-year periods were $7.5 million or less
   e. Once the corporation fails the gross receipts test, the corporation becomes subject to the AMT prospectively
3. Adjustments applicable only to corporations
   a. The adjusted current earnings (ACE) adjustment applies only to corporate taxpayers. This adjustment was designed to ensure that all corporations pay some minimum tax on economic income.
   b. The ACE adjustment is equal to 75% of the difference between ACE and AMTI. ACE is essentially economic income.

> **EXAMPLE** XBA Corp has AMTI of $200,000 before any ACE adjustment. The corporation has adjusted current earnings of $300,000. Therefore, the ACE adjustment is $75,000 [($300,000 – $200,000) × 75%]. The $75,000 would be added to the AMTI before the ACE adjustment in arriving at a total adjusted AMTI of $275,000.

4. Some AMT adjustments are not applicable to corporations (only applicable to individuals)
   a. Adjustments for itemized deductions, standard deductions, and personal exemptions of individuals
   b. Adjustments for incentive stock options
   c. Adjustments for qualified small business (Section 1202) stock
5. Calculation of AMTI for a corporation:

	Taxable income
+	Positive AMT adjustments
–	Negative AMT adjustments
+	Tax preferences
=	AMTI before ACE adjustment
+	ACE adjustment
=	Alternative minimum taxable income

6. Calculation of AMT for corporations:

	AMTI
–	AMT exemption ($40,000 if available)
=	Minimum tax base
×	AMT rate (20%)
=	Tentative AMT
–	Regular income tax on taxable income
=	AMT

E. CREDITS ALLOWED AGAINST AMT

For 2011, the list of nonrefundable credits allowable against AMT was incomplete. Please login to the AccFP 104 course at **www.schweser.com/cfp** and refer to the Updates & Errata link for 2011 updates released subsequent to printing.

XVII. TAX CREDITS

A. TAX CREDITS

1. Generally dollar-for-dollar reductions of the income tax liability of the taxpayer
2. Provide benefits on a more equitable basis than tax deductions; credits are not affected by the tax rate of the taxpayer

B. OVERVIEW AND PRIORITY OF CREDITS

1. Refundable tax credits are paid to the taxpayer even if the amount exceeds the taxpayer's tax liability (creates a refund)
2. Nonrefundable tax credits—at best, the tax liability can be reduced to zero. If the taxpayer has multiple nonrefundable tax credits, they must be offset using the priority list defined in the Code. Some credits are subject to carryover provisions (e.g., foreign tax credit).
    a. Does not create a refund

C. GENERAL BUSINESS CREDITS

1. Rehabilitation expenditures credit
    a. Tax credit allowed to rehabilitate industrial and commercial buildings and certified historic sites and is set up to discourage businesses from moving to newer locations
    b. Subject to limits based on the taxpayer basis in the property and other conditions
2. Energy credit—10% of taxpayer's basis in qualified energy property placed in service during the tax year (generates energy from a solar or geothermal source)
    a. Certain property may be eligible for a 30% investment credit
3. Work Opportunity Tax Credit (WOTC)
    a. Employers may elect a credit against their tax liability for wages paid to members of one or more of eight targeted groups who begin work before September 1, 2011
    b. Subject to limitations on the amount of the credit and a percentage limitation
4. Research activity credit
    a. This credit is the sum of the incremental research credit and the basic research credit
    b. Incremental research credit—the Code does not specifically list what research activities qualify. However, it does state what is not allowed.
    c. Basic research credit—this credit applies to C corporations but not S corporations or personal service corporations and allows qualifying corporations to take an additional 20% credit for basic research payments
5. Low-income housing credit
    a. This credit is available to qualified low-income housing projects. One requirement for qualification is to have the property certified under such a title.
    b. If the property continues to qualify, the credit has a 10-year life

6. Disabled access credit
   a. The credit is 50% of the eligible access expenditures over $250 but not more than $10,250 [maximum credit equals ($10,250 – 250) × 50%, or $5,000]
   b. Only eligible small businesses can claim the disabled access credit. An eligible small business is a business with $1 million or less in gross receipts and 30 or fewer full-time employees.
   c. The credit applies to any qualifying project (e.g., installation of ramps and raised markings on routine usage items)
   d. If the credit is used, the adjusted basis for that piece of property is reduced by that same amount
7. Foreign tax credit—the corporate taxpayer may either deduct the foreign income taxes paid or accrued or make an election to claim the foreign taxes as a credit against its US income tax liability (IRS Form 1118)

D. PERSONAL CREDITS

1. Earned income credit (EIC)
   a. The credit is designed to encourage economically disadvantaged individuals to join the work force
2. Credit for the elderly or disabled
   a. This limited, nonrefundable credit applies to taxpayers 65 and older or those under 65 who are retired and permanently or totally disabled
   b. The spouses must have lived apart the entire year to qualify for the credit as MFS; otherwise, to receive the credit, married couples must file MFJ
3. Foreign tax credit
   a. The foreign tax credit is a means of avoiding double taxation by granting a tax credit for taxes paid or accrued to a foreign country or a US possession
   b. A taxpayer may not take advantage of both the foreign tax credit and the foreign earned income exclusion
   c. If the tax in the foreign jurisdiction is more than the US tax, taking the tax credit is generally more advantageous
4. Child and dependent care credit
   a. This credit is allowed for a portion of child or dependent care expenses paid for the purpose of allowing the taxpayer to be gainfully employed
   b. For eligibility, the taxpayer must have earned income (both husband and wife in the case of married couples), must be paying the child- or dependent-care expenses to be able to work or look for work, and must keep a home for a qualifying individual. A qualifying individual is any of the following:
      1.) A dependent under age 13 for whom a dependency exemption may be claimed
      2.) Any other person who is physically or mentally incapable of caring for himself and lives with the taxpayer for more than half of the year. In this case, the taxpayer must either (1) be able to claim the person as a dependent or (2) be

able to claim the person as a dependent except for the fact that the person had income exceeding the exemption amount.

3.) The taxpayer's spouse who is physically or mentally incapable of self-care and lives with the taxpayer for more than half of the year

4.) Certain dependent children of divorced parents

c. Household services, in addition to expenses for the care of the children, can be included to determine the credit amount

d. For 2011, the employment-related expenses eligible for the credit are limited to $2,400 for one qualifying child and $4,800 for two or more qualifying children

e. To calculate the credit, multiply the work-related expenses by a percentage (which depends on gross income)

EXHIBIT 24: Child and Dependent Care Credit for 2011

		Maximum Credit	
Adjusted Gross Income	Credit Rate	One Child	Two or More Children
$10,000 or less	30	720	1,440
10,001 – 12,000	29	696	1,392
12,001 – 14,000	28	672	1,344
14,001 – 16,000	27	648	1,296
16,001 – 18,000	26	624	1,248
18,001 – 20,000	25	600	1,200
20,001 – 22,000	24	576	1,152
22,001 – 24,000	23	552	1,104
24,001 – 26,000	22	528	1,056
26,001 – 28,000	21	504	1,008
28,001 and over	20	480	960

5. Adoption credit

a. In 2011, the adoption credit is a refundable credit for qualified adoption expenses (nonrefundable for tax years 2012 and beyond). The maximum credit is $13,360 (for 2011) per eligible child, including children with special needs.

b. The credit is taken in the year the adoption becomes final. Any unused credit may be carried forward up to five years.

c. The credit is phased out beginning at modified AGI of $185,210, with complete phaseout at $225,210

6. Child tax credit

a. For 2011, a $500 credit is given for each qualifying child under age 17

b. Qualifying child includes child, stepchild, grandchild, or eligible foster child. In any case, the child must be a dependent.

c. Credit is reduced $50 for each $1,000 above threshold

Status	AGI Threshold
Married filing jointly	$110,000
Single or head of household	$75,000
Married filing separately	$55,000

d. The child tax credit is a refundable credit

7. Hope Scholarship Credit
   a. Available for qualified tuition expenses (tuition and fees) incurred and paid in the first two years of postsecondary education in a degree or certificate program for taxpayer, spouse, or dependent
      1.) Room and board are not qualifying expenses
      2.) Qualifying expenses must be reduced by any tax-free income, and taxpayers cannot use the same educational expense for figuring more than one benefit
   b. The credit is 100% of first $1,200 of qualified expenses paid in the tax year plus 50% of the next $1,200; maximum of $1,800 for the tax year
   c. Calculated on a per student basis
   d. Student must carry at least half of normal load during one term
   e. A convicted drug felon is not eligible
8. Lifetime Learning Credit
   a. Available for tuition and fees (undergraduate, graduate, or professional degree programs)
   b. May claim 20% of qualified expenses up to $10,000
   c. Maximum of $2,000 credit per year per tax return. Note that maximum is family based, unlike the Hope Scholarship Credit.
   d. Student must be enrolled at least half time in a degree or certificate program
   e. If courses are taken to acquire or improve job skills, student can be enrolled less than half time
   f. Credit can be claimed for an unlimited number of years
   g. Cannot claim both the Hope Scholarship Credit and Lifetime Learning Credit for the same individual in the same year. However, it would be possible to take the Hope Scholarship Credit and the Lifetime Learning Credit on the same return if there are two students in the family (each qualifying individually).
   h. Taxpayers may claim a Hope Scholarship Credit or Lifetime Learning Credit for a taxable year and exclude from their gross income any amounts distributed (both the contributions and the earnings portions) from a Coverdell Education Savings Account on behalf of the same student, as long as the distribution is not used for the same educational expenses for which a credit was claimed

EXHIBIT 25: MAGI* Phaseout for Hope Scholarship and Lifetime Learning Credits for 2011

Hope Scholarship and Lifetime Learning Credits	
Married filing jointly	$102,000–$122,000
All other taxpayers	$51,000–$61,000

*MAGI—AGI and foreign earned income exclusion and US possessions and Puerto Rico income exclusions

EXHIBIT 26: Highlights of Tax Benefits for Higher Education for 2011

	Hope Scholarship Credit	Lifetime Learning Credit	Coverdell Education Savings Account[1]	Traditional and Roth IRAs[1]	Student Loan Interest	Qualified Tuition Programs (Section 529 Plans)	Education Savings Bond Program[1]
What is your benefit?	Credits can reduce the amount of tax you must pay		Earnings are not taxed	No 10% additional tax on early withdrawal	You can deduct the interest	Earnings are not taxed	Interest is not taxed
What is the annual limit?	2011 Up to $1,800 per student	2011 Up to $2,000 per family	$500 contribution per beneficiary	Amount of qualifying expenses	2011 $2,500	None	Amount of qualifying expenses
What expenses qualify besides tuition and required enrollment fees?	Course materials	None	Books Supplies Equipment Room and board if at least a half-time student Payments to qualified tuition program	Books Supplies Equipment Room and board if at least a half-time student	Books Supplies Equipment Room and board Transportation Other necessary expenses	Books Supplies Equipment Room and board if at least a half-time student	Payments to Coverdell ESAs Payments to qualified tuition programs
What education qualifies?	First 2 years of under-graduate	All undergraduate and graduate[2]					
What are some of the other conditions that apply?	Can be claimed only for 2 years. Must be enrolled at least half-time in a degree or certificate program.		Can also contribute to qualified tuition programs in the same year Cannot contribute after 18th birthday of beneficiary Must withdraw assets at age 30		For 2011, available only for first 60 months. Must have been at least half-time student in a degree program.	Distribution is excluded from gross income. Hope Scholarship and Lifetime Learning Credits are permitted in the same year but not for the same expenses.	Applies only to qualified Series EE bonds issued after 1989 or Series I bonds
In what income range do benefits phase out?	2011 Single $51,000–$61,000 MFJ $102,000–$122,000	2011 Single $51,000–$61,000 MFJ $102,000–$122,000	2011 Single $95,000–$110,000 MFJ $150,000–$160,000	No phaseout[2]	2011 Single $40,000–$55,000 MFJ $60,000–$75,000	No phaseout	2011 Single $71,100–$86,100 MFJ $106,100–$136,100

[1] Any nontaxable withdrawal is limited to the amount that does not exceed qualifying education expenses.

[2] Phaseouts exist at time of contribution. They are not relevant for withdrawals.

EXAMPLE (Assume a taxpayer marginal tax rate of 25% or higher)

	Example 1			Example 2		Example 3	
Short-term	Short-term capital gain	$4,000		$3,000		$1,000	
	Short-term capital loss	2,000		9,000		5,000	
		$2,000	Gain (short-term capital gain)	$6,000	Loss (short-term capital loss)	$4,000	Loss (short-term capital loss)
28% Long-term	Gain	$3,000		$4,000		$2,000	
	Loss	9,000		1,000		1,000	
		$6,000	Loss (long-term)	$3,000	Gain (long-term)	$1,000	Gain (long-term)
25% Long-term		$0		$1,000	Gain (long-term)	$2,000	Gain (long-term)
20%/10% and 18%/8% Long-term	Gain	$13,000		$4,000		$2,000	
	Loss	9,000		1,000		1,000	
		$4,000	Gain (long-term)	$3,000	Gain (long-term)	$1,000	Gain (long-term)
Net	Net	$2,000	Short-term capital gain	$6,000	Short-term capital loss	$4,000	Short-term capital loss
		$2,000	Long-term capital loss (28%)	$7,000	Long-term capital gain	$4,000	Long-term capital gain
Final net		$0	Gain or loss	$1,000	Long-term capital gain 20%/10% or 18%/8%, depending on the holding period and the taxpayer's tax bracket	$0	Gain or loss

NOTE: Ending up with both gains and losses is not possible.

D. DETERMINING GAIN OR LOSS—SUMMARY

1. The realized gain or loss is calculated by reducing the amount realized by the adjusted basis of the property
   a. If the amount realized exceeds the adjusted basis, a gain results
   b. If the amount realized is less than the adjusted basis, a loss occurs

2. The recognized gain/loss is reported on the tax return
   a. Any individual taxpayer's gain or loss that is not currently recognized is either deferred (postponed) or excluded (disallowed)
   b. Corporations have a limited option to carry back capital losses for three years in addition to a limited carry forward of five years

E. DETERMINING GAIN OR LOSS

1. Realized gain or loss
   a. Trade-ins, casualties, condemnations, thefts, and bond retirements are treated as dispositions of property.
   b. Amount realized
      1.) This is the sum of any money received, plus the FMV of other property received, plus real property taxes owed by the seller but paid by the buyer, plus any liability on the property assumed by the buyer (e.g., mortgage or some other liability—second mortgage, lien)
      2.) The FMV of property received in a sale or other disposition is defined as the price at which property will change hands between a willing seller and a willing buyer, both with knowledge of relevant facts, when neither is compelled to buy nor sell
2. Adjusted basis
   a. Adjusted basis is the property's original basis adjusted to the date of disposition (cost + capital additions – capital recoveries) = adjusted basis

> **EXAMPLE** Harold bought a building for $20,000 cash and assumed a mortgage of $80,000. Harold's basis in the building is $100,000.

3. Capital recoveries—there are many forms of capital recoveries, but the most widely known are depreciation, casualties, and theft
4. Capital additions—cost of capital improvements made to the property by the taxpayer (not including ordinary repair and maintenance)
5. Sales, exchange, or condemnation of personal-use assets. Realized losses associated with personal-use assets are not recognized. Exception: casualty or theft losses. In contrast, realized gains may be fully taxable.

F. RECOVERY OF CAPITAL DOCTRINE

1. This doctrine allows taxpayers to recover the cost or other original basis of property acquired, free from tax. For example, the cost or other basis of depreciable property is recovered through annual depreciation deductions.
2. Recognition of gain can sometimes be postponed (deferred gain)
   a. For example, a like-kind exchange under Section 1031 or an involuntary conversion under Section 1033 is eligible for postponement treatment

3. A realized loss that is never recognized (disallowed loss) results in the permanent recovery of less than the taxpayer's cost or other basis for tax purposes
   a. For example, a loss on the sale of a personal-use asset is not deductible
4. A realized loss where recognition is postponed (postponed loss) results in the temporary recovery of less than the taxpayer's cost or other basis for tax purposes

G. DETERMINATION OF BASIS OF PROPERTY RECEIVED FROM A SALE

1. Basis is generally the property's cost—the amount paid for in cash or other property. Exception: a bargain purchase has a cost basis equal to its FMV (logic: bargain element would have been included in income).
2. Lump-sum property purchases—the lump-sum cost is allocated between the properties on the basis of their respective FMVs

> **EXAMPLE** Scott bought a tract of land for $20,000 and subdivided the land into 10 building lots of equal size. If Scott sold all 10 lots individually, his basis in each would be $2,000.

3. Property received as compensation for services is generally includable in the taxpayer's gross income at fair market value (FMV), which becomes the taxpayer's basis in the property

H. DETERMINATION OF BASIS AND HOLDING PERIOD WHEN PROPERTY IS RECEIVED BY GIFT

1. A gift indicates no cost to the recipient. However, a basis to the gifted property is still assigned and depends on the following:
   a. The date of the gift
   b. The donor's adjusted tax basis of the property gifted
   c. The amount of gift tax paid (if any) by the donor
   d. The FMV of the property on the date of the gift
2. Gift of appreciated property
   a. When the donor gives appreciated property to the donee, generally the basis to the donee is the carryover basis of the donor. The donee's basis is the donor's old basis.
   b. The donor's holding period carries over to the donee
   c. A realized gain occurs if the donee subsequently sells the gifted property at a higher price than the property's adjusted basis
   d. If the donor paid gift tax at the time the appreciated property is gifted, the donee can increase his basis by a portion of the gift taxes paid. The following formula is used to determine a donee's basis when the donor has paid gift taxes:

$$\text{Donee's basis} = \text{donor's adjusted basis} + \left(\frac{\text{unrealized appreciation}}{\text{FMV} - \text{donor's annual exclusion amount used for the gift}}\right) \times \text{gift tax paid}$$

EXAMPLE Chelsea gave Virginia stock with an FMV of $60,000 and paid gift tax of $15,000. Chelsea had originally acquired the stock two years ago for $20,000. The annual exclusion amount had already been used for a prior gift to Virginia by Chelsea. Virginia's basis in the gift is $30,000, calculated as follows:

Answer:

$$\$20,000 + \left[\frac{40,000}{60,000}\right] \times 15,000 = \$30,000 \text{ basis}$$

Basis includes $20,000 of carryover basis, plus $10,000 of the gift tax paid. Virginia immediately has a holding period of two years, which is the carryover holding period from Chelsea.

If the annual exclusion had been available for the gift, the calculation would have been:

$$\$20,000 + \left[\left(\frac{\$40,000}{\$60,000 - \$13,000}\right) \times \$15,000\right] = \$32,766 \text{ basis in the gift}$$

3. Gift of loss property
   a. When the donor gives loss property to the donee, the double basis rule applies
   b. Basis cannot be determined until the donee subsequently disposes of the gifted property
      1.) Gain basis
         a.) If the donee subsequently disposes of the property at a higher price than the donor's adjusted tax basis, the donee determines the gain according to the donor's basis (carryover basis)
         b.) The donor's holding period also carries over to the donee in determining whether the gain is short term or long term
         c.) If the donor paid gift tax at the time of the gift, the gift tax is not allocated to the donee's basis when the property is subsequently disposed of
      2.) Loss basis
         a.) If the donee subsequently disposes of the property at a lower price than the FMV of the property at the time of the gift, the donee determines the loss on the basis of the FMV at the time of the gift
         b.) The donor's holding period does not carry over to the donee in determining whether the loss is short term or long term. The donee's holding period begins on the date of the gift.
         c.) If the donor paid gift tax at the time of the gift, the gift tax is not allocated to the donee's basis when the property is subsequently disposed of
      3.) If the donee sells the gifted property at a price between the donor's adjusted tax basis and the FMV at the date of the gift, no gain or loss is recognized at the time of the sale

> **EXAMPLE** Bill received an acre of land as a gift from his father. When the gift was made, the land had an FMV of $700,000. His father purchased the land four years ago for $800,000 and paid gift tax of $100,000. Assume Bill sold the land one week after receiving the gift:
>
> - If Bill sold the land for $850,000, he would have a long-term capital gain of $50,000 ($850,000 – $800,000) on the sale. Bill would use his father's carryover basis of $800,000 (gain basis) and would use his father's carryover holding period of four years. Gift tax paid by his father will not be allocated to Bill's basis because this was a gift of loss property.
> - If Bill sold the land for $550,000, he would have a short-term capital loss of $150,000 ($550,000 – $700,000) on the sale. Bill's basis would be the $700,000 FMV on the date of the gift (loss basis), and Bill's holding period would begin on the date of the gift. Gift tax paid by his father would not be allocated to Bill's basis because this was a gift of loss property.
> - If Bill sold the land for $730,000, there would be no gain or loss because he sold the land at a price between his father's adjusted tax basis and the FMV at the date of the gift. The holding period is irrelevant due to no gain or loss.

I. BASIS OF PROPERTY RECEIVED FROM A DECEDENT

1. For years ending December 31, 2009, and also for years beginning January 1, 2011, when receiving property from a decedent, the basis of such property is the FMV at the date of death or, if the alternate valuation date is properly elected, the FMV up to six months after the date of death. However, there are restrictions on electing the alternate valuation date.
2. Alternate valuation date limitations
   a. An estate tax return must be filed
   b. Both the value of the gross estate and the estate tax liability must be reduced to less than what the primary valuation date would have yielded
   c. The alternate valuation date is six months after the date of death, unless the property is disposed of before six months after the date of death, in which case the valuation is the disposition value
3. Deathbed gifts
   a. If appreciated property is given to a donee who then dies within one year and bequeaths the previously gifted property back to the donor, the basis of the inherited property will be the donor's adjusted basis at the time of the gift to the decedent. No step-up in basis is received.

> **EXAMPLE** Joey gives property to his father in the current year that has an FMV of $7,000 on the date of the gift. No gift taxes were paid. Joey has an adjusted basis in the property of $2,300. Joey's father dies at the end of the current year and bequeaths the property back to Joey within one year of the date of the gift. Joey's basis in the property is $2,300 (donor's basis).

4. Survivor's share of property (joint tenants with right of survivorship)
    a. The basis of such property is the FMV at the date of the decedent's death for the portion related to the decedent. This figure is added to the survivor's basis.

> **EXAMPLE** Martin and Mary owned, as joint tenants, land that they purchased for $60,000. At the date of Mary's death in 2011, the property had an FMV of $100,000. Local law states that joint tenants each have a half interest in the income for jointly held property. Martin figures his basis in the property as follows:
>
> | | |
> |---|---|
> | Interest Martin bought up front | $30,000 |
> | Interest Martin received at Mary's death | $50,000 |
> | Martin's basis after Mary's death | $80,000 |
>
> Only the portion of the property inherited by the surviving owner receives a step-up in basis in common-law states.

5. The holding period of property acquired from a decedent is always deemed to be long term. This provision applies whether the property is disposed of at a gain or loss.
6. Community property receives an adjustment in basis to FMV on both halves at the death of the first spouse
7. Note: For property received from a decedent whose death occurred in 2010, the Economic Growth and Tax Relief Reconciliation Act of 2001 (EGTRRA) repeals the step-up in basis rules
    a. Because the estate tax is also repealed for deaths occurring in 2010, there is also no gross estate
    b. When receiving property from a decedent, the carryover basis of the property to the beneficiary is the lesser of:
        1.) the adjusted basis of the property at the decedent's date of death; or
        2.) the FMV on the date of death
    c. The decedent's estate can elect to increase the basis of up to $1.3 million of property passing to beneficiaries
        1.) A further increase the basis of an additional $3 million of property passing to the surviving spouse
        2.) Total of $4.3 million of property can receive a stepped-up basis in an estate
    d. Jointly owned property
        1.) Surviving owner is the decedent's spouse
            a.) Property which was held by the decedent and surviving spouse as joint tenants with right of survivorship or as tenants by the entireties, one-half of the property is eligible for a step up in basis
            b.) Upon the death of the first spouse joint tenant, the surviving spouse can receive a step-up in basis to FMV on 50% of the property:
                - up to $3 million in assets, if available and elected by the executor; or

- if the $3 million has been used for other assets, the lesser of the FMV at the date of death or the decedent's adjusted basis in the property which is added to the surviving spouse's original 50% basis

2.) Surviving owner is a nonspouse

a.) Only the portion of the property representing the decedent's contribution is eligible for the step-up in basis election

- The basis of property for which the decedent's estate can demonstrate contribution to the purchase is the FMV at the date of the decedent's death for the portion related to decedent, if the $1.3 million allowance is applied to the asset; otherwise, it is the lesser of the FMV at the date of death or the decedent's adjusted basis in the property

b.) This amount is added to the survivor's basis

EXAMPLE Mark owns a house he purchased several years ago for $50,000. When the value of the house increased to $150,000, he added his daughter's name to the title as JTWROS.

- If Mark predeceased his daughter in 2010, the daughter's basis in the house could be 100% (and not just her 50% share) of:
  - the FMV of the entire property at Mark's date of death (if elected by the executor); or
  - the lesser of the FMV of the entire property at the date of death or the decedent's adjusted basis in the property.
- If Mark's daughter predeceased Mark in 2010, the daughter's estate or Mark must be able to sufficiently prove that the entire purchase price was provided by Mark.
- If Mark had added his spouse's name to the title as JTWROS, instead of his daughter's, each spouse would be deemed to have contributed 50% of the purchase price of the house. Upon death of the first spouse in 2010, the survivor's basis would be $100,000 ($25,000 purchase price + $75,000 FMV of decedent's share of the house) if the $3 million allowance for the step-up in the basis of assets passed to a surviving spouse had not yet been fully used.

NOTE: Because there was no estate tax in 2010, there is no need to calculate what amount would be included in the gross estate of a decedent.

e. Community property

1.) Both halves would be eligible for the additional basis allocation (up to a total of $3 million) to FMV at the death of the first spouse

2.) If, in the previous example, Mark and his spouse lived in a community property state and the house had been held as community property, the surviving spouse's new basis could be $150,000 at the death of the first spouse in 2010 (based on the availability of the $3 million exception)

J. HOLDING PERIOD EXCEPTIONS

1. Generally, property must be owned longer than a year to be treated as long-term property
2. Gift property—if the donor's basis carries over to the donee, the donor's holding period is added (tacked on) to the donee's holding period
3. Inherited property—the property is treated as long term regardless of the actual original holding period
4. Capital asset or Section 1231 asset—in a like-kind exchange between a capital asset or Section 1231 asset, the newly acquired property includes the holding period of the former property
5. Mark to market rules
    a. Applies to Section 1256 contracts
        1.) Regulated futures contracts
        2.) Foreign currency contracts
        3.) Nonequity options, such as S&P 500 Index option
        4.) Dealer equity options
    b. Any Section 1256 contracts must be marked to market at year end, and any gain or loss must be reported. The effect is to treat the contract as if it were sold on the last day of the taxable year.
    c. Capital gain or loss is treated as 40% short term and 60% long term. Gain is adjusted by any amounts considered in previous years and is reflected in adjustment to basis.

K. DISALLOWED LOSSES

1. Related taxpayers—losses from sales to related parties are disallowed
    a. Related parties include brothers, sisters, and lineal descendants (they stop at and do not include cousins); corporations in which the taxpayer has a 50% or greater interest; and several other complex relationships
    b. However, if the subsequent sale of the property by the recipient results in a gain, this gain can be reduced by the previously disallowed loss. The related buyer's holding period begins on the date of the purchase from the related party.

> **EXAMPLE** Dave sells stock to his son for $70 on January 1, 2011. Dave's adjusted tax basis was $100, and Dave purchased the stock on February 4, 2001. Dave's loss of $30 is disallowed, and Dave will never benefit from the loss.
>
> On June 2, 2011, his son sells the stock to an unrelated party for $115. His gain is $15 ($115 – $70 = $45 – $30 = $15). His son was able to allocate Dave's disallowed loss to his gain.

2. Wash sales
    a. A wash sale occurs if the taxpayer sells or exchanges stock or securities for a loss and, within 30 days before or after the date of the sale or exchange, acquires similar securities

b. If such an event occurs, the basis of the new stock or securities will include the unrecovered portion of the basis of the formerly held stock or securities

EXAMPLE Tiffany purchased 100 shares of Ace Corporation stock for $28,000 on January 1 of last year. In the current tax year, she sold 30 shares of these 100 shares for $8,000. Twenty-nine days earlier, she purchased 30 shares for $7,500.

Tiffany's recognized loss is $0, calculated as follows:

Amount realized	$8,000	
Adjusted basis (30 × $280)	(8,400)	
Realized loss	(400)	
Recognized loss	$0	(Loss postponed because of wash sale rule)

Her basis in the new shares is $7,900:

Purchase price new shares	$7,500
Add postponed loss	400
Basis in new shares	$7,900

3. Conversion of personal property to business property or income-producing property
   a. If converted, the basis for loss is the lower of the property's FMV on the date of conversion or the adjusted basis
   b. The basis for gain is the property's adjusted basis
   c. The basis for depreciation is the same as the basis for loss, explained previously

L. INSTALLMENT SALES

1. In general
   a. The general rule of taxation is that all gains are recognized in the year of sale or exchange. An exception to this rule applies to the installment sale method of accounting.
   b. An installment sale is any sale of property (see following exceptions) in which the seller will receive at least one payment after the close of the tax year in which the sale occurs
   c. The installment-sale method allows the taxpayer to spread out the gain as the payments are received
   d. The installment-sale method is automatic for sales that qualify. However, the taxpayer is allowed to elect out of this method by reporting the entire gain in the year of sale.
2. Installment treatment is not available for
   a. property held for sale in ordinary course of business (inventory); or
   b. gains on stocks or securities traded in an established market

3. Tax ramifications of installment sales

   a. The reported gain is based on the amount of cash received and the gross-profit percentage resulting from the sale

      1.) Section 1245/1250 recapture rules—gain recaptured under either Section 1245 (depreciable personal property used in a trade or business) or gain recaptured as the excess of accelerated depreciation over straight-line depreciation is taxed as ordinary income (Section 1250 depreciable real property used in a trade or business) and is not eligible for installment sale treatment

         a.) These amounts are fully recognized (taxable) as ordinary income in the year of sale

         b.) The ordinary income recognized in the year of sale is added to the property's basis, and this adjusted basis is used in determining gross profit in the sale

         c.) If a portion of the gain on an installment sale are attributable to 25% gain (straight-line depreciation on real property) and another consists of 20%/18% gain, the taxpayer must recognize the 25% gain before the 20%/18% gain when reporting gain received from installment sale payments

         d.) As a planning technique, it may not be advisable to sell some types of depreciable property used in a trade or business using the installment method

> **EXAMPLE (Calculating Adjusted Basis in an Installment Sale with Recapture)** Carol sells a building with an adjusted basis of $30,000 for $100,000. Carol has taken $15,000 of depreciation on the property, of which $5,000 is subject to recapture as ordinary income. Carol includes the $5,000 as ordinary income in the year of sale. The $5,000 is added to her adjusted basis to determine her gross profit on the sale. Gross profit is $100,000 – $35,000 = $65,000 gain on the sale. Carol's remaining gain consists of a return of basis of $35,000, Section 1250 recapture of $10,000, and capital gain of $55,000. When she receives installment payments, each payment will consist of 35% return of basis and 65% capital gain. She will be taxed at the 25% rate on the first $10,000 of capital gain she receives in the payments, not recognizing the capital gain at the 20%/18% rate until she has been taxed on all of the recaptured 25% gain.

      2.) The gross-profit percentage is calculated by subtracting the seller's adjusted tax basis from the total contract price and dividing that figure by the contract price

> **EXAMPLE** Mike sold a 40-acre tract of land for $500,000 on January 1. The land had an adjusted basis of $300,000. The agreement specified a down payment of $100,000, with the remaining $400,000 sales price to be paid over a five-year-note term at 10% interest. The gross profit from the sale is $200,000 ($500,000 – $300,000), and the gross-profit percentage is 40% ($200,000 profit ÷ $500,000 sales price).

3.) Down payment—the down payment received from an installment sale is partially a capital gain and partially a return of capital. The capital gain portion is based on the amount of cash received and the gross-profit percentage calculated previously.

> **EXAMPLE** Assume the same facts as above. The down payment of \$100,000 received by Mike is reported as a \$40,000 capital gain and a \$60,000 return of capital. The capital-gain portion is calculated by multiplying the down payment by the gross-profit percentage (\$100,000 down payment × 40% gross-profit percentage = \$40,000). The remaining \$60,000 of the down payment will be considered a nontaxable return of capital.

4.) Note payments—the note payments received from the buyer are partially ordinary income, partially capital gain, and partially a return of capital

a.) If a portion of the gain on an installment sale is attributable to 25% gain (straight-line depreciation on real property) and another consists of 20%/18% gain, the taxpayer must recognize the 25% gain before the 20%/18% gain when reporting gain received from installment sale payments

> **EXAMPLE** Assume the same facts as above. Mike received a note payment of \$120,000 in the first year, of which \$40,000 represented accrued interest. Therefore, the note payment represented \$40,000 of interest and \$80,000 of principal repayment. The note payment would be reported as \$40,000 ordinary income, \$32,000 capital gain (\$80,000 principal payment × 40% gross-profit percentage), and \$48,000 nontaxable return of capital (\$80,000 principal payment x 60% nontaxable return of capital).

4. Other provisions of installment sales

a. Gains recaptured as ordinary income under Sections 1245 and 1250 (depreciable property) are not eligible for installment-sale treatment. These amounts are fully recognized as ordinary income in the year of sale and are added to the basis of the property being sold.

b. If the selling price is more than \$3,000 and the contract does not have a reasonable rate of interest, interest will be imputed

c. If property is sold to a related party and the related party sells the property to a third party within two years, the deferred gain must be recognized in full by the original seller

d. If an installment obligation is sold or otherwise disposed of, any unreported gain must be reported in the year the note was transferred

M. SALES OR EXCHANGES—SPECIAL ISSUES

1. Worthless securities—if the securities are capital assets, they will be treated as being disposed of or sold on the last day of the tax year
2. Options—if the option is a capital asset, the grantee will realize a capital gain or loss upon sale or exchange. If the grantee fails to exercise the option, the sale or exchange will be considered to have occurred on the expiration date.
3. Short sales
   a. Taxpayer anticipates a decline in the price of stock and sells it short
   b. Taxpayer sells stock he has borrowed and repays it with substantially identical property (either already owned or purchased after the sale)

> **EXAMPLE** Gina has been watching the market carefully and decides that Pearl Computer is not going to make its target quarterly income. In anticipation that the stock price will decline, Gina sells 100 shares of Pearl (borrowed from her broker) for $10,000. In 60 days, Gina purchases 100 shares for $8,000 and repays her broker, closing the short sale. Gina made $2,000 on the transaction.

   c. The term *short sale against the box* refers to a short sale in which the seller borrows stock but actually already owns the same stock

> **EXAMPLE** Gina already owned 100 shares of Pearl but borrowed 100 shares from her broker. To close the short sale, she delivers the shares she already owns. The advantage is that she has more flexibility in reporting when the sale occurs.

   d. Nature of the gain: if the stock is a capital asset to the taxpayer, the gain or loss is capital
      1.) If the taxpayer has not held substantially identical securities for the required long-term holding period at the date of the short sale or the substantially identical property is acquired between the short-sale date and the closing date, any gain or loss is short term
      2.) If substantially identical property has been held for the long-term holding period on the short-sale date and it is used to close the sale, the gain is long term
      3.) If substantially identical property has been held for the long-term holding period on the short-sale date and a loss occurs, it is considered long term whether or not the substantially identical property was used to close the sale
   e. Constructive sale rules—reduce the reporting flexibility for short sales against the box. If a taxpayer does not close a short position by January 31 in the year following the short sale, a constructive sale is deemed to have been made on the earlier of (1) the short-sale date (if the taxpayer owned substantially identical securities at that time) or (2) when the taxpayer acquired substantially identical securities during the year of the short sale.
   f. At the time of printing, Congress had allowed the qualified dividend tax rate to sunset
      1.) Dividend income is taxable at ordinary income tax rates for 2011

XIX. PROPERTY TRANSACTIONS—NONTAXABLE EXCHANGES

A. GENERAL

1. The tax law recognizes that nontaxable exchanges result in a change in the form but not in the substance of the taxpayer's relative economic position. The replacement property received in the exchange is substantially viewed as a continuation of the old investment.
2. In a nontaxable exchange, realized gains or losses are not recognized except to the extent of boot received in the transaction (see Like-Kind Exchanges—Section 1031 below). However, this nonrecognition is usually temporary because the gain or loss is postponed. This is accomplished by assigning a carryover basis to the replacement property.

B. LIKE-KIND EXCHANGES—SECTION 1031

1. In general
   a. Section 1031 provides for nontaxable exchange treatment if the following requirements are satisfied
      1.) The form of the transaction is an exchange
      2.) Both the property transferred and the property received are held either for productive use in a trade or business or for investment
      3.) The property is like-kind property
2. Like-kind property
   a. The words *like-kind* refer to the nature or character of the property and not to its grade or quality. One kind or class of property may not be exchanged for property of a different kind or class.
   b. The following properties or exchanges are not considered like-kind
      1.) Personal-use assets (personal auto)
      2.) Ordinary assets (inventory)
      3.) Securities
      4.) Personalty exchanged for realty. Depreciable tangible personal property must be within the same general business asset class or the same product class (e.g., office furniture, information systems, automobiles, and trucks).
      5.) Livestock of different sexes
      6.) Foreign real estate for domestic real estate
3. Exchange requirement—the transaction must actually involve an exchange of property to qualify as a like-kind exchange
4. Boot
   a. Boot is property received in an exchange that is not like-kind property
   b. Boot includes the following
      1.) Cash received

2.) Liabilities assumed by the other party from the original taxpayer

3.) Other non-like-kind property, such as personal property received in an exchange involving real property

c. The receipt of boot will result in:

1.) the recognition of gain if there is a realized gain; or

2.) no recognition if there is a realized loss

d. Exception: if the boot is appreciated or depreciated property, the gain or loss is recognized to the extent of the difference between the FMV and adjusted basis of the boot

EXAMPLE Bob exchanged investment land with an adjusted basis of $35,000, receiving another parcel of investment land with an FMV of $50,000 plus $12,000 in cash. As a result of this exchange, Bob will have a realized (economic) gain of $27,000 and a recognized (taxable) gain of $12,000.

FMV of property received	$50,000
Cash (boot) received	$12,000
Amount realized	$62,000
Less adjusted basis of asset surrendered	(35,000)
Equals realized gain	$27,000
Recognized gain (lesser of realized gain or boot received)	$12,000

EXAMPLE Bob exchanged investment land with an adjusted basis of $55,000, receiving another parcel of investment land from Steve with an FMV of $50,000. Bob's land was subject to a $15,000 mortgage, which was assumed by Steve. As a result of this exchange, Bob will have a realized (economic) gain of $10,000 and a recognized (taxable) gain of $10,000.

FMV of property received	$50,000
Cash (boot) received	$15,000
Amount realized	$65,000
Less adjusted basis in asset surrendered	(55,000)
Equals realized gain	$10,000
Recognized gain (lesser of realized gain or boot received)	$10,000

The mortgage assumed by Steve represents boot to Bob.

5. Multiple properties

a. An exchange may involve more than one property

b. When multiple properties are involved, the various business assets are matched with those of the same kind

6. Basis and holding period of property received

a. The basis of like-kind property received in the exchange is the property's FMV less deferred gain or plus postponed loss and is also called the property's substituted basis. If the exchange partially qualifies for nonrecognition (if recognition is associated with boot), the basis of like-kind property is the property's FMV less postponed gain or plus postponed loss. The basis of any boot received is the boot's FMV.

b. An alternative approach for determining the basis of like-kind property received is as follows:

	Adjusted basis of like-kind property surrendered
+	Adjusted basis of boot given
+	Gain recognized
–	FMV of boot received
–	Loss recognized
=	Basis of like-kind property received

EXAMPLE (Like-Kind Exchange) Pat exchanges real estate (adjusted basis $50,000, FMV $80,000) held for investment for other real estate (FMV $80,000) held for investment. Pat's basis in the new property is $50,000.

EXAMPLE (Partially Nontaxable Exchange) Craig trades in a truck (adjusted basis $6,000) for a new truck (FMV $5,200) and also receives $1,000 in cash. Craig's basis in the new truck is:

Adjusted basis of old truck	$6,000
Cash received	($1,000)
Gain recognized ($6,200 – $6,000)	$200
Basis of new truck	$5,200

c. The holding period of the property surrendered in the exchange carries over and adds to the holding period of the like-kind property received

d. The boot's holding period starts from the date of exchange and is not considered a carryover holding period

7. Other requirements

a. If like-kind property is exchanged with a related party, the taxpayer and related party must not dispose of the like-kind property received in the exchange within a two-year period following the exchange. Exceptions: death and involuntary conversions.

b. The property to be received in an exchange must be identified in a written agreement within 45 days after the transferred property is surrendered

c. Property in the exchange must be received on or before the earlier of:

1.) 180 days after the transfer of the property given up; or

2.) the due date of the tax return (including extensions) for the year the property was given up

C. INVOLUNTARY CONVERSIONS—SECTION 1033

1. An involuntary conversion results from the destruction (complete or partial), theft, seizure, requisition, condemnation, or sale or exchange under threat or imminence of requisition or condemnation of the taxpayer's property
2. Section 1033 allows a taxpayer who incurs an involuntary conversion to postpone recognition of gain realized from the conversion. The rules for nonrecognition are as follows:
    a. If the amount reinvested in replacement property equals or exceeds the amount realized, the realized gain is not recognized
    b. If the amount reinvested in replacement property is less than the amount realized, the realized gain is recognized to the extent of proceeds not reinvested
3. Typically, the amount realized from the condemnation of property is equal to the amount received as compensation for the property. Severance damages are usually not included in the amount realized.
4. Replacement property
    a. The general requirement is that the replacement property is similar in service or use to the involuntarily converted property. For an owner-user, the functional use test applies, and for an owner-investor, the taxpayer use test applies.
        1.) Functional use test—the taxpayer's use of the replacement property and of the involuntarily converted property must be the same. For example, an office building used as an office building by the owner is subject to an involuntary conversion. The replacement property must be an office building used as an office building.
        2.) Taxpayer use test—the owner-investor's properties must be used in similar endeavors as the previously held properties. This test is more flexible than the functional use test. For example, if the owner had held the office building as an investment property, the replacement property could be any realty investment property.
5. Time limitation on replacement
    a. Normally, the taxpayer has a two-year period from the end of the taxable year in which any gain is realized from the involuntary conversion to replace the property. Exception: condemnation of real property used in a trade or business or held for investment has a three-year period.
    b. The earliest date for replacement is typically the date the involuntary conversion took place
6. Nonrecognition of gain may be either mandatory or elective, depending on the disposition/conversion of the replacement property (whether it was money or similar property)
    a. Direct conversion—if converting to replacement property, nonrecognition of realized gain is mandatory. The basis of the converted property is the same as the replacement property. Direct conversion is rare in practice.
    b. Conversion into money—if the conversion is into money, nonrecognition is elective. The basis of the replacement property is the property's cost less postponed (deferred)

gain. If postponement is elected, the holding period of the replacement property includes the holding period of the converted property.

c. Section 1033 applies only to gains, not losses

EXAMPLE Bill had some property condemned by the State of Louisiana. The property had an adjusted basis of $26,000. Bill received $31,000 from the state for the property. Bill just realized a gain of $5,000 ($31,000 – $26,000) and bought new property that was similar in use to his old property for $29,000. He must recognize a gain of $2,000 ($31,000 – $29,000). Bill's basis in his new property is as follows:

Cost of new property	$29,000
Gain not recognized (deferred gain)	($3,000)
Bill's basis in the new property	$26,000

7. Involuntary conversion of a personal residence
   a. The tax consequence depends on whether a casualty or condemnation occurred and if it produced a realized loss or gain
   b. Loss circumstances
      1.) If the conversion is a condemnation, the realized loss is not recognized
      2.) If the conversion is a casualty, the realized loss is recognized subject to the personal casualty loss limitations
   c. Gain circumstances
      1.) If the conversion is a condemnation, the gain may be postponed under either Section 1033 or, if qualifying, excluded under Section 121
      2.) If the conversion is casualty, the gain is only postponed under the involuntary conversion provisions

D. SALE OF A PERSONAL RESIDENCE—SECTION 121

1. Section 121 gives a universal exclusion of up to $250,000 (married filing jointly, $500,000) to any taxpayer who meets certain use tests
   a. Home must have been owned and used as a principal residence for at least two of the five years before the sale (do not have to be consecutive years)
   b. Either spouse can meet the ownership requirement, but both must meet the use requirement. Neither spouse can be ineligible because of the once-every-two-year limit in c.
   c. Exclusion can be used once every two years
   d. If taxpayer fails to meet the ownership and use tests because of a change in employment or health, the taxpayer may be entitled to a partial exclusion based on the shorter of either use or ownership
   e. If one spouse can take the full exclusion and one cannot, the exclusion is the sum of the amounts calculated on a separate basis as if they had not been married

f. The exclusion does not apply to gain attributable to post May 6, 1997, depreciation for business or rental use of the house

g. Taxpayers who deferred gain under the older Section 1034 provisions may add on the old residence's use and ownership period to the new residence

EXAMPLES

- Gloria, a single taxpayer, sold her condominium in Seattle because she has a new job in Detroit. On the sale date, she had owned the condo for only 18 months. Gloria failed to meet both the use and ownership tests because of a change in employment, so she receives a partial exclusion: (18 months ÷ 24 months) × $250,000 = $187,500.
- If Gloria had lived in the condo for two years but had only owned it for one year (she rented for a year before she purchased it), proposed regulations specify that the shorter of the two periods should be used. Her partial exclusion would be: (12 months ÷ 24 months) × $250,000 = $125,000.
- Merrily and Wallace get married, and Wallace moves into the house that Merrily has been using as her principal residence for six years. Nine months later, Wallace gets a big promotion and the newlyweds move to another city. They realize a $700,000 gain on the sale of their residence. Merrily meets both the ownership and use tests. She gets a full exclusion of $250,000. Wallace does not need to meet the ownership test (because his wife did), but he is held to the use test. He has only been there nine months, so his exclusion is (9 ÷ 24) × $250,000 = $93,750. Their total exclusion is $250,000 + $93,750 = $343,750.
- If Wallace and Merrily had just moved to a larger house in the same city, Merrily would get her $250,000 exclusion (she has met all tests, and it has been at least two years since she claimed an exclusion), but Wallace would not get an exclusion. Remember that the partial exclusion is only allowed if the sale is necessitated by a change in employment or health.

2. When selling a personal residence, like any other personal asset, losses are not recognized
3. The Housing Assistance Act of 2008 restricts the use of the home sale exclusion for periods of nonqualified use even though the two-out-of five-year ownership and use tests are otherwise satisfied

    a. Meant to prevent conversion of rental property or vacation home to principal residence and use of the exclusion again in two years after sale of principal residence

    b. Nonqualified use is any period after December 31, 2008, for which the property is not used as the principal residence, and includes:

        1.) periods the taxpayer remodels the residence and does not live in it

        2.) rental and vacation home usage of the residence

    c. If nonqualified use exists, the total realized gain from the sale of the residence must be allocated between qualified and nonqualified use

        1.) Gain allocated to periods of nonqualified use is the total amount of gain multiplied by a fraction:

            a.) the numerator is the aggregate of periods of nonqualified use during the period the property was owned by the taxpayer; and

            b.) the denominator is the period the taxpayer owned the property

2.) Denominator includes entire ownership period while the numerator includes only periods after December 31, 2008

3.) Periods of use after the taxpayer moves out of the home are not considered as nonqualified use but are still part of the five-year ownership period. This period cannot exceed three years.

EXAMPLE Barney's filing status is single and he is in the 25% marginal tax bracket. He purchased a residence March 1, 2009, as a rental property, subsequently claiming $20,000 of depreciation. After two years, Barney moved into the home and used it as his principal residence until March 2, 2013. His adjusted tax basis was $380,000 on March 1, 2011. He moved out of the home March 2, 2013. Barney sold the home March 2, 2014, for $700,000.

Barney's gain on the sale of the property is $320,000 ($700,000 – $380,000). He has Section 1250 depreciation recapture of $20,000 which will be taxed at a 25% rate. Total ownership of the home is five years and there are two years of nonqualified use. To calculate how much of the gain qualifies for the exclusion and how much is allocated to nonqualified use, multiply the remaining gain of $300,000 × 40% (2 years ÷ 5 years), therefore, $120,000 ($300,000 × 40%) of the gain will be taxed as long-term capital gain. The remaining $180,000 ($300,000 – $120,000) of gain is eligible for the home sale exclusion. Barney can exclude all of the $180,000 of qualified gain as it does not exceed his $250,000 exclusion amount. As a result of this sale, the $320,000 of total realized gain will be taxed as follows:

$20,000 taxed at the 25% capital gains rate (depreciation recapture under Section 1250)

$120,000 taxed at the long-term capital gains rate (gain relating to nonqualified use)

$180,000 gain excluded from gross income (Section 121 exclusion applies)

d. Exceptions to nonqualified use

1.) Qualified official duty: members of uniformed services, Foreign Service, or intelligence community (aggregate period of less than 10 years)

2.) Temporary absence exception: due to change in employment, health conditions, or other unforeseen circumstances specified by the IRS (aggregate periods less than two years)

4. The Mortgage Forgiveness Debt Relief Act of 2007

a. Allows a surviving single spouse to qualify for the up-to-$500,000 exclusion if the sale occurs no later than two years after the other spouse's death and the requirements for the $500,000 exclusion under Section 121 were met immediately before the spouse's death

b. Effective for sales and exchanges after Dec. 31, 2007

EXAMPLE Martha and Howard were married and had lived in their home for 40 years when Martha died on February 1, 2010. The couple owned the home as joint tenants with rights of survivorship and had an adjusted cost basis of $100,000. The FMV at the date of Martha's death was $500,000. Howard's adjusted cost basis was increased to $300,000. There was no nonqualified use of the home. On November 10, 2011, Howard accepted an offer from a developer of $800,000 for the property which is in a highly desirable location. Because Howard sold the personal residence within two years of Martha's death, he may exclude all of the gain on the sale of the home as a surviving spouse and is not limited to the $250,000 gain of a single taxpayer.

A. SALES OF STOCK

1. The basis will be the purchase price of the stock plus any commissions or fees associated with the purchase. Basis may be subsequently adjusted for nontaxable stock dividends, stock splits, or nontaxable distributions that are a return of capital.
2. Basis options when selling
   a. First in, first out (FIFO) is the default
   b. Specific identification (only if indicated at the time of the sale)
3. Gain will be calculated as net sales proceeds (amount realized) less adjusted basis
4. A sale will result in a capital gain or loss unless sold for basis
5. Cash dividends are includable in taxable income
   a. Dividends are paid from corporate earnings and profits

B. BONDS—CORPORATE OR TREASURY

1. Income (interest) is taxable
2. The sale of a bond creates a capital gain or loss if disposed of at an amount different from basis
3. If a corporate bond is bought at a premium, the taxpayer will reduce the basis by the amount of amortization taken (if elected)
4. Treasury bond interest is not subject to state income tax

C. MUNICIPAL BONDS

1. The interest on municipal bonds is tax exempt for federal tax purposes
2. The sale of a municipal bond creates a capital gain or loss if disposed of at an amount different from basis
3. Premiums on municipal bonds must be amortized, and the basis must be reduced by the amortized amount. No deduction is taken for the amortization on municipal bonds.
4. Original issue discount (OID) on tax-exempt bonds—while exempt from federal income tax, the OID must be accrued and added to the taxpayer's basis in the bond in order to determine gain or loss upon disposition of the bond

D. ORIGINAL ISSUE DISCOUNT (OID) BONDS—CORPORATE OR TREASURY

1. OID typically applies to zero-coupon or deep-discount bonds
2. Interest is usually accrued and includable in income in spite of an absence of cash flow
   a. Often referred to as phantom income—income that is taxable but not received in cash or property at the time of recognition for income tax purposes
3. The sale of an OID bond will result in capital gain or loss if the sale proceeds are different from the adjusted tax basis
4. The accrued interest reported each year by the taxpayer is added to the basis

E. EMPLOYEE STOCK OPTIONS

1. Usually given by employer as a form of compensation
2. Gives taxpayer the right to buy company's stock at a certain price within a specified time frame
3. Generally, no income is recognized when the option is granted
4. The amount and timing of income recognition depends on the type of stock option awarded
    a. Nonqualified stock options (NQSOs)
        1.) Individual will recognize income when the NQSO is granted, if the option is traded on an exchange and not subject to a substantial risk of forfeiture. An example of substantial risk of forfeiture is a requirement that the employee not exercise the option for a year.
        2.) Individual is taxed on the bargain element when the option is exercised (the difference between the FMV of the stock on the date of exercise and the option price)
        3.) The bargain element is taxed at ordinary income tax rates and will be included in the employee's W-2
        4.) Any appreciation that occurs after the date of exercise is taxed as a capital gain
        5.) Basis is the FMV at date of exercise
        6.) The holding period begins on the date of exercise, which determines if the gain is long term or short term
    b. Incentive stock options (ISOs)
        1.) No income is recognized when the option is granted
        2.) No regular tax is due when the option is exercised
        3.) Tax is due when the stock is subsequently sold
            a.) If the taxpayer does not dispose of stock within two years after the option grant and holds the stock for more than one year (after exercise), any gain over the exercise price will be capital gain
            b.) If the taxpayer sells the stock within one year after the exercise date, the gain is treated as ordinary income
        4.) AMT may require earlier recognition of income because the difference between the option price and the FMV at date of exercise is an addback for AMT purposes

EXAMPLES

- John's employer grants him an NQSO with an exercise price of $25. John exercises the NQSO when the market value is $40. The $15 difference is included in John's W-2 income and is subject to FICA and FUTA. If John sells the stock two years later for $60, his basis in the stock is $40 and he has a long-term capital gain of $20.
- George's employer grants him an ISO on January 1, Year 1, with an exercise price of $25. George exercises the ISO on January 2, Year 2, when the market price is $40. No ordinary income recognition is triggered, but $15 will be an AMT adjustment. George sells the stock two years later for $60, his basis is $25, and he has a $35 long-term capital gain for regular tax.

NOTE: His AMT basis is $40, and AMT gain is $20.

F. MUTUAL FUNDS

1. Most mutual funds distribute income and capital gains
2. Taxation of mutual funds
    a. Capital gains earned by mutual fund
        1.) If the capital gain is distributed to the shareholder in cash, the shareholder will be taxed on the capital gain and will not be permitted to increase his adjusted tax basis in the mutual fund shares
        2.) If the shareholder elects to automatically reinvest the capital gain, the shareholder will still be taxed on the capital gain but is permitted to increase his adjusted tax basis in the mutual fund shares
        3.) Capital gain distributions are taxed at favorable long-term capital gain rates (IRS Publication 564)
    b. Dividends earned by mutual fund
        1.) If the dividend is distributed to the shareholder in cash, the shareholder will be taxed on the dividend and will not be permitted to adjust his tax basis in the mutual fund shares
        2.) If the shareholder elects to automatically reinvest the dividend, the shareholder will still be taxed on the dividend but is permitted to increase his adjusted tax basis in the mutual fund shares
    c. Sale of mutual fund shares by shareholder
        1.) When a shareholder sells mutual fund shares, a capital gain or loss will result
            a.) The gain or loss is determined by subtracting the shareholder's adjusted tax basis from the sale price
            b.) The shareholder has the following options in determining basis of the shares sold
                - FIFO
                - Average cost per share
                - Specific identification (must identify shares before the sale)

c.) If a shareholder recognizes a capital gain from the sale of mutual fund shares, the capital gain can be offset by any capital losses from the sale of other securities. Conversely, if a shareholder recognizes a capital loss from the sale of mutual fund shares, the capital loss can be offset by any capital gains from the sale of other securities.

EXAMPLE Tommy purchased a mutual fund with a $10,000 lump-sum amount two years ago. He elected to reinvest all dividends and capital gains. Last year, the mutual fund paid a dividend of $500 and had a capital gain distribution of $200. During the current year, the mutual fund paid a dividend of $700 and had capital gain distribution of $300. Today, Tommy sold all of the mutual fund shares for $20,000.

This year, Tommy will report dividend income of $700 and capital gains of $300 on his personal income tax return, even though the dividend and capital gains were reinvested.

Tommy's basis in the mutual fund shares is $11,700 ($10,000 original cost + $500 + $200 + $700 + $300). Because he was taxed on the dividends and capital gains over the two-year holding period, he will be entitled to increase his basis in the mutual fund shares.

Tommy will have a capital gain of $8,300 ($20,000 sales price – $11,700 basis) resulting from the sale of the mutual fund shares. This capital gain can be offset by any capital losses Tommy incurs from the sale of other securities.

G. PERSONAL-USE PROPERTY

1. The sale of personal-use property at a gain will generally be a capital gain
2. The loss on a sale of personal-use property is nondeductible

H. SECTION 1244 STOCK

1. Losses on Section 1244 stock are ordinary losses up to $50,000 per year for single taxpayers and up to $100,000 for married taxpayers filing jointly
2. Any excess losses beyond the $50,000 or $100,000 as applicable in the year are capital losses (subject to offsetting other capital gains and limited to $3,000)
3. Gains from the sale of Section 1244 stock are capital gains

I. EXCHANGE OF E OR EE BONDS FOR HH BONDS

1. If a cash-basis taxpayer did not make the election to currently report interest on held Series E or EE bonds, he may have exchanged these bonds for Series HH bonds without recognizing any of the deferred interest on the E or EE bonds
2. The basis of the E or EE bonds carries over, and when the HH bonds are redeemed, the deferred interest is then recognized

XXII. BUSINESS ORGANIZATIONS

NOTE: Additional information is in Appendix 5.

A. LEGAL FORMS OF BUSINESS ORGANIZATIONS

1. Sole proprietorship—a business owned by only one individual, who is personally liable for the obligations of the business
2. General partnership—an association of two or more persons, who jointly control and carry on a business as co-owners for the purpose of making a profit
   a. The partners are personally liable for the obligations of the business
3. Limited partnership—a partnership in which at least one partner is a general partner and at least one partner is a limited partner
   a. A limited partner does not participate in management and has limited liability
4. Limited liability partnership (LLP)—usually a professional partnership (e.g., Certified Public Accountants, attorneys) in which the partners have limited liability to the extent of investment except where personally liable through malpractice
   a. This form protects the individual assets of the nonmalpracticing partners
5. Limited liability company (LLC)—an entity in which the owners (members) have limited liability for debts and claims of the business even while participating in management
   a. The governing document is called an operating agreement
   b. Some states prohibit single-member LLCs
6. Corporation—a separate legal entity that is created by state law and operates under a common name through its elected management
   a. Owners (shareholders) have limited liability
7. S corporation—a corporation with no more than 100 shareholders, restricted to citizens and resident aliens, certain estates or trusts, and no more than one class of stock

B. SOLE PROPRIETORSHIPS

1. A sole proprietorship is a business owned and controlled by one person who is personally liable for all debts and claims against the business
2. Advantages of sole proprietorships
   a. No separate entity (simplicity)
   b. Not costly to establish
   c. Can respond quickly to business opportunities
   d. Easy to terminate business
3. Disadvantages of sole proprietorships
   a. Not easy to raise capital
   b. Unlimited liability
   c. Proprietorship will probably terminate upon death or incapacity of proprietor

4. Taxation of sole proprietorships
    a. Income from the sole proprietorship is taxed directly to the proprietor, who must include a Schedule C in his individual tax return (Form 1040)
    b. Neither the formation nor the termination of a proprietorship is a taxable event
    c. To terminate sole proprietorship
        1.) Cease operations
        2.) Pay off all vendors
        3.) Final income or loss reported on Schedule C of Form 1040

C. GENERAL PARTNERSHIPS

1. Characteristics of a general partnership are found in partnership law (the law of agency)
    a. The elements of a general partnership
        1.) A common ownership interest in an ongoing business
        2.) A sharing of profits and losses of the business
        3.) A right to participate in the management and operation of the business
    b. A partnership is treated as an entity, separate and apart from its individual members for certain purposes
        1.) The partnership has the capacity to sue and be sued in the name of the partnership (state laws vary)
        2.) Judgments can be entered against a partnership in its name
        3.) The partnership is subject to liquidation proceedings under federal bankruptcy laws
        4.) The partnership can participate in transfers and ownership of personal and real property (state laws vary)
    c. A partnership may be treated as an aggregate under federal laws and some state laws
2. Formation of partnership
    a. No special state filings are required in forming a general partnership
    b. The contribution of money or property to a partnership, in exchange for a partnership interest, is a nontaxable transaction
    c. Basis in partnership interest
        1.) A partner's basis in the partnership interest begins with contributions and is subsequently adjusted by earnings and losses
            a.) Cash contribution—basis equal to the value of the cash contributed
            b.) Property contribution—carryover basis
        2.) Distributions to partners will reduce basis
        3.) A partner's basis is also decreased by any share of his liabilities assumed by the partnership

3. Taxation of partnerships
    a. Partnerships are flow-through entities for purposes of federal income taxation
    b. Items of income and deduction, which occur at the partnership level, will not be taxed to the partnership. Instead, those items of income and deduction will be reported to the partner on his individual federal income tax return (Form 1040).
    c. Income and deductions will flow through to the partner and retain their character. Items that flow through separately and retain their character include the following:
        1.) Income and loss items (e.g., ordinary income, rental income, capital gain income)
        2.) Deductions (e.g., charitable contributions, Section 179 expense)
        3.) Credits (e.g., low-income housing, rental real estate)
        4.) Investment interest
        5.) Self-employment
        6.) Adjustments and tax preference items (e.g., depreciation, depletion)
        7.) Foreign taxes
        8.) Other (e.g., tax-exempt interest income, distributions of property or money, nondeductible expenses)
    d. These items of income and deduction are reported on Schedule K of the Federal Partnership Return (Form 1065) and will be reported to the partners on Schedule K-1
        1.) Each partner will receive a Schedule K-1 that includes his share or allocation of each item of income and deduction
        2.) The sum of all Schedules K-1 will equal the amount reported on Schedule K
    e. Each of the separately stated items on Schedule K-1 will be reported in the appropriate place on the partner's individual federal income tax return (Form 1040)
        1.) For example, interest and dividends are reported on Schedule B
4. Termination of partnership—occurs following the dissolution and winding up (liquidation) of a partnership
    a. Dissolution occurs when a partner ceases to be associated with the partnership business, resulting in a change in the relation of the partners, or by admission of a new partner (results in dissolution of the former partnership and the creation of a new one). The new partnership is liable for the obligations of the old partnership.
        1.) Dissolution by operation of law
            a.) Death of a partner
            b.) Bankruptcy of the partnership or a partner (in most cases)
            c.) Illegality, which makes it unlawful to continue the business or continue with one of the partners

2.) Dissolution by judicial decree

a.) Upon application of a partner

b.) Upon application of third party (e.g., assignee or creditor of a partner)

b. Winding up

1.) Dissolution terminates the authority of partners, except the authority to complete unfinished business

a.) Unfinished business includes collecting, preserving, and selling partnership assets, discharging liabilities, collecting debts owed to the partnership, allocating current income, and accounting to each other for the value of their interests in the partnership

b.) If the partnership is insolvent, partnership's creditors have priority over individual's creditors with respect to partnership assets

- The partnership's creditors may then look to partners' assets
- If a partner is insolvent, the order of payment is (1) partner's creditors and then (2) partnership creditors

2.) Taxation at dissolution

a.) In general

- When dissolution occurs, the partnership's taxable year closes with respect to all its partners
- If partners use different taxable years than the partnership, a bunching of income may occur

b.) Liquidating distributions

- When a partnership liquidates, the liquidating distributions made to a partner usually consist of an interest of several partnership assets
- The partner may be required to recognize gain on the distribution
- The calculation of gain is based on a set of distribution ordering rules
  - Cash is considered distributed first. The partner will recognize gain to the extent the cash received exceeds his basis in the partnership interest.
  - The partner's remaining basis is then allocated to inventory and receivables
  - Any additional basis is then allocated to the other assets received by the partner
- If the partner received only money, receivables, or inventory, the partner will be allowed to recognize a loss if the partner's basis in the partnership interest exceeds the partner's basis in the assets distributed
- The partnership itself typically does not recognize gain or loss on liquidating distributions

D. LIMITED PARTNERSHIPS

1. Formation
   a. The partners sign a certificate including, but not limited to, the firm name, nature and duration of business, and names of partners
   b. The certificate is filed with the designated state or local official
   c. The contribution of money or property to the partnership, in exchange for a partnership interest, is a nontaxable transaction
   d. Basis in partnership interest
      1.) A partner's basis in the partnership interest begins with contributions and is subsequently adjusted by earnings and losses
         a.) Cash contribution—basis equal to the value of the cash contributed
         b.) Property contribution—carryover basis
      2.) Cash or property distributions to partners will reduce basis
      3.) A partner's basis is also decreased by any share of his liabilities assumed by the partnership
2. Liability of partners to creditors
   a. A limited partner is liable to creditors only to the extent of that partner's contributed or promised capital
   b. A general partner has unlimited personal liability to creditors
3. Rights of a partner
   a. A limited partner (member) has no authority to bind the partnership; however, a general partner has such authority
   b. A limited partner and general partner have the same rights as partners in a general partnership with respect to suing, examining books, accounting, the return of partner's capital contribution, and the assignments of rights to partner's interest
4. Taxation of limited partnerships
   a. Limited partnerships are taxed under the same concepts as a partnership
5. Dissolution
   a. By acts of parties
      1.) Expiration of term in which the partnership was formed
      2.) If the partnership is not formed for a specified term, the will of a general partner
      3.) Withdrawal or expulsion of a general partner unless otherwise provided in the certificate or unless members consent to continuation
   b. By operation of law
      1.) Death or insanity of a general partner if the business cannot be continued in accordance with certificate or consent of other members
      2.) Illegality
      3.) Bankruptcy of firm or a general partner

c. Limited partner's withdrawal, death, assignment of interest, or bankruptcy (unless it causes the bankruptcy of the firm) does not result in the dissolution of the firm

d. Winding up and liquidation procedure, following dissolution, is the same as that for a general partnership except for the priorities in distribution

e. The Uniform Limited Partnership Act specifies the following order for distribution of the partnership's assets

   1.) Outside creditors

   2.) Limited partners' shares of profit and any other compensation

   3.) Limited partners' return of capital contributions

   4.) Advances and loans made by general partners

   5.) General partners' shares of profits

   6.) General partners' return of capital contributions

f. The Revised Uniform Limited Partnership Act changes the order by including claims of partners, who are creditors, with outside creditors and combining limited and general partners

E. FAMILY LIMITED PARTNERSHIP (FLP)

1. Introduction

a. A partnership with a general partner and at least one limited partner

b. Generally designed to address several purposes:

   1.) Convenient administration of investments, while retaining control

   2.) A vehicle for annual gifts for transfer tax planning purposes

   3.) Provide for creditor protection for limited partners

c. Typically created by a senior family member who transfers business or investment assets to the partnership

   1.) General partner has significant control over the business activities of the partnership, makes investment and management decisions, and determines when distributions should be made to the limited partners

   2.) Often, the senior family member serves as general partner

d. The partnership agreement will govern how partnership income is divided among the partners

   1.) Generally, both general and limited partners share income and cash flow on the basis of their percentage interest in the partnership

   2.) The taxable income of the FLP is reported annually and allocated to each partner on the basis of that partner's percentage interest

   3.) The allocation is noted on the Schedule K-1 issued to each partner

   4.) Usually, the general partner distributes annually at least enough cash to pay the income tax liability attributable to each partner

e. Distributions are not taxable to the extent the partner has basis in the partnership interest

   1.) The partnership itself (unlike a corporation) is not subject to tax because it passes through all items of income and deduction to the partners

   2.) Limited partners also have restrictions on their ability to transfer their partnership units to others so that the general partners can prevent the units from being transferred outside of the family

2. Advantages

   a. The FLP has significant impact in reducing a transferor's gift and potential estate tax

      1.) By using an FLP, the owner can take advantage of gift and estate tax valuation rules relating to minority interests and marketability that can reduce transfer taxes

      2.) Because of the significant restrictions imposed on the limited partnership units, the partnership units typically will have a value approximately 30% less than the value of the assets originally transferred to the partnership

      3.) Actual discounts can range from 25–60%

   b. Besides reduced asset values for estate and gift tax purposes through significant valuation discounts, other benefits include the following:

      1.) Ability of the general partners to make substantial gifts yet maintain control of the partnership assets

      2.) Continuing control of income from transferred assets because distributions from an FLP must be authorized by general partners

      3.) Identification of partnership assets as separate assets and not marital assets. This would be important in the event of a divorce.

      4.) Control of the future investment of family assets and retention of a critical mass to enhance future investment opportunities

      5.) Reduced probate costs with respect to real estate located in other states. No ancillary administration is required.

      6.) Institutionalization and enhancement of family communication on family business and investment matters

F. CORPORATIONS

1. Nature of corporations

   a. Business corporations are artificial, legal entities whose creation and operations are controlled by state statutes

   b. A corporation is regarded as a person who is separate from the shareholders

      1.) The capacity of a corporation to sue and be sued in the name of the corporation

      2.) The protection against self-incrimination (restricted to natural persons)

      3.) Criminal liability

      4.) Licensing statutes

c. Shareholders

1.) Shareholders are generally the holders of ownership interests in the corporation and may freely transfer their interests

2.) Death of a shareholder does not dissolve or otherwise affect the corporation

3.) Shareholders enjoy limited liability (amount of their investment) and are not personally liable for the debts of the corporation

4.) Shareholders have equitable interests in, but not legal title to, corporate property

5.) Shareholders do not represent the corporation but vote for the board of directors, which determines corporate policy and appoints officers. The officers represent the corporation.

6.) Shareholders may sue and be sued by the corporation, and they may deal with the corporation in arm's-length transactions

d. Tax considerations

1.) The profits of a corporation are taxed to the corporation at special corporate rates

2.) Distributions of profits, in the form of dividends, are treated as taxable income to the recipients and are not deductible by the corporation (double taxation of profits)

3.) If shareholders sell their shares, they are taxed on any gains (long- or short-term capital gains rates)

2. Special taxes applicable to C corporations

a. In general

1.) The following special taxes apply exclusively to C corporations

a.) Personal holding company tax

b.) Personal service corporation tax

c.) Accumulated earnings tax

2.) These taxes are paid by the C corporation

3.) Dividends-received deduction refers to a reduction in the amount of a dividend received by a corporation based on its ownership in another corporation

a.) If the dividend-receiving corporation owns less than 20% of the dividend-paying corporation, the dividends-received deduction will be 70% of the dividend actually received

b.) If the dividend-receiving corporation owns at least 20% of the dividend-paying corporation, but less than 80%, the dividends-received deduction will be 80% of the dividend actually received

c.) If the dividend-receiving corporation owns at least 80% of the dividend-paying corporation, the dividends-received deduction will be 100% of the dividend actually received

b. Personal holding company tax

1.) The objective of the personal holding company tax is to discourage individual taxpayers from using the corporate entity solely for tax avoidance

2.) Applies only if the corporation is considered a personal holding company and has undistributed personal holding company income

3.) A corporation will be considered a personal holding company if it meets both of the following tests:

a.) Ownership test—during the last half of the taxable year, greater than 50% of the value of the outstanding stock of the corporation is owned by five or fewer individuals

b.) Passive income test—at least 60% of the corporation's adjusted ordinary gross income consists of personal holding company income

- Adjusted ordinary gross income is the company's gross income, with several adjustments. Adjustments include reductions for property taxes, depreciation, and interest expense.
- Personal holding company income is generally defined as passive income and certain income from services

c.) Undistributed personal holding company income is the corporation's adjusted taxable income, less the dividends paid deduction

4.) The tax is calculated by multiplying the undistributed personal holding company income by the applicable personal holding company tax rate (not determined for 2011 as of publication date)

a.) The personal holding company tax is levied in addition to the regular tax

b.) The tax can be avoided by distributing the personal holding company income as dividends to the shareholder(s)

c.) Corporations not subject to the personal holding company tax:

- S corporations
- Life insurance companies
- Banks
- Certain other financial institutions

c. Personal service corporation tax

1.) Personal service corporations are corporations that meet the following requirements:

a.) Involved in fields of health, law, engineering, architecture, accounting, actuarial science, performing arts, or consulting

b.) At least 95% of the stock is held by active or retired employees

2.) Income earned by a personal service corporation is taxed to the corporation at a special rate, which has not been determined for 2011 by the date of publication

d. Accumulated earnings tax

1.) The objective of the accumulated earnings tax is to discourage individual taxpayers from using the corporate entity solely for tax avoidance

2.) The tax applies whenever a corporation accumulates earnings beyond its reasonable needs, unless the corporation can prove to the contrary by a preponderance of evidence

3. Taxation at liquidation

a. In general

1.) For tax purposes, a liquidation occurs when a corporation is no longer a going concern

2.) A complete liquidation is taxed as a sale or exchange to the shareholder. This treatment is similar, but not identical, to the tax treatment of a qualified stock redemption.

b. Effect on shareholder

1.) The shareholders are treated as having sold their stock to the liquidating corporation

2.) The shareholders may recognize gain or loss

3.) The gain or loss recognized is calculated as the difference between the FMV of the property received from the corporation and the adjusted basis of the shareholders' stock

c. Effect on corporation

1.) A liquidating corporation may or may not be required to recognize gain or loss, depending on the nature of the transaction

2.) Generally, the corporation is required to recognize gain or loss upon complete liquidation

a.) The gain or loss is calculated as if the corporation's assets were sold at FMV

b.) Losses may be disallowed in certain circumstances

- If the distribution is made to certain related parties, the loss may be disallowed
- If the distribution is made with certain built-in loss property, the loss may be disallowed

G. S CORPORATIONS

1. Taxation of S corporation shareholders

a. In general, the IRS treats S corporation shareholders as partners

1.) Shareholders of S corporations are required to report pro rata shares of corporate items that flow through

2.) Although partnerships have great flexibility in the allocation of income and deductions, this advantage is not available to S corporations

3.) All items of income are reported on the basis of the ownership percentage of each shareholder

b. The principal advantage of S corporation status is the avoidance of the double taxation of dividends associated with C corporation status

c. Generally, an S corporation must be a calendar year taxpayer, unless it can establish a business purpose for adopting a fiscal year to the satisfaction of the IRS

d. For purposes of the Code's fringe benefit provisions, an S corporation is treated as a partnership, and a shareholder-employee who owns more than 2% of its stock is treated as a partner

1.) The value of benefits provided to a more than 2% shareholder-employee must be included in that shareholder's gross income unless the Code specifically allows exclusion of the benefit by a partner

2.) Accident and health insurance premiums paid by an S corporation for a more than a 2% shareholder-employee are deductible by the corporation

3.) Included in the shareholder's gross income

4.) The entire amount included in income may be deducted by the shareholder-employee

2. Election

a. Requirements for S corporation election—must be deemed a small business corporation

1.) The entity must be organized under the laws of any US state or territory

2.) Shareholders may be individuals, estates, certain trusts, or certain tax-exempt organizations

a.) Partnerships and corporations may not be shareholders

b.) A grantor, voting trust, or testamentary trust may be an eligible shareholder for two years after the deemed owner's death

c.) Exempt organizations such as qualified pension plans, profit-sharing plans, stock bonus plans, and charitable organizations may also be shareholders

3.) Only citizens or residents of the United States may be shareholders

4.) The entity may only have one class of stock issued and outstanding

a.) The rights of the holders must be identical with regard to profits and assets of the corporation

b.) Two classes are permitted if the only difference is voting rights

5.) The entity may have no more than 100 shareholders

a.) A married couple (as well as certain families) is considered one shareholder regardless of how they hold their shares

b. How to make the election

1.) S corporation status is elected by having all shareholders consent and file Form 2553 by the 15th day of the third month of the tax year in which the shareholders wish the election to take effect

2.) The corporation must meet all of the eligibility requirements in the preelection period of the tax year in which the shareholders want the election to take effect

3. Special taxes applicable to S corporations

a. In general

1.) Although S corporations are flow-through entities, they may be required to pay one of the following taxes:

a.) Built-in gains tax

b.) LIFO recapture tax

c.) Excess net passive income tax

2.) These taxes are paid by the S corporation, not by the shareholders

b. Built-in gains tax

1.) The built-in gains tax applies to S corporations that used to be C corporations

2.) This tax is imposed on any unrealized built-in gain that is recognized on the disposition of any asset by the S corporation

a.) The unrealized built-in gain is the difference between the FMV and the basis of an asset as of the date the C corporation converts to an S corporation (conversion date)

b.) The recognized built-in gain is any gain recognized from the sale of an asset within the 10-year period following the S corporation election

c.) Any assets acquired by the S corporation after the conversion date are not subject to the built-in gains tax

d.) Any appreciation of the asset after the date of conversion is not subject to the built-in gains tax

3.) The Small Business Jobs Act of 2010

a.) Temporarily shortened the built-in gain holding period to five years

b.) No built-in gains tax is imposed if the fifth tax year in the recognition period preceded the 2011 tax year

> **EXAMPLE** Eli Corporation converts from a C corporation to an S corporation effective January 1, 2006. It has an office building with a large gain built in at the time of conversion. If Eli corporation sells the building in 2011, the built-in gains tax will not apply, as the five year period has passed.

c.) Tax does not apply to corporations that first made the S corporation election at the time of incorporation and never operated as C corporations

4.) The tax is computed by applying the highest corporate income tax rate to the S corporation's net recognized built-in gain for the tax year

5.) The amount of recognized built-in gain passed through and taxed to shareholders is reduced by the built-in gains tax paid by the S corporation

c. LIFO recapture tax

1.) The LIFO recapture tax applies to S corporations that used to be C corporations

2.) A C corporation that uses the LIFO method of inventory valuation in its last taxable year before making an S corporation election must include in income a LIFO recapture amount

a.) The LIFO recapture amount is the excess of the inventory valuation under the FIFO method over the inventory valuation under the LIFO method

b.) The recapture amount is reported in the taxable income of the C corporation in its last tax year

c.) The inventory's basis is increased by the LIFO recapture amount

> **EXAMPLE** StaceCo converted from a C corporation to an S corporation. On the date of the conversion, StaceCo had inventory with a LIFO basis of $90,000. The FIFO value of the inventory was $140,000. StaceCo must add a $50,000 ($140,000 – $90,000) LIFO recapture amount to its last C corporation tax return.

3.) The LIFO recapture tax is the tax on the LIFO recapture amount

a.) The tax is calculated on the basis of the corporation's ordinary income tax rate

d. Excess net passive income tax

1.) The excess net passive income tax applies to S corporations that used to be C corporations

2.) The S corporation must pay a tax on its excess net passive income if passive investment income exceeds 25% of its gross receipts during the year

a.) Passive investment income is generally gross receipts derived from royalties, rents, dividends, interest, annuities, and gains from sales of securities

b.) Net passive income is passive investment income reduced by any allowable deduction directly connected with the production of such income

4. Revocation and termination of S corporation status

a. This election may be revoked by the consent of more than half of the corporate shareholders (including nonvoting) and may specify a particular date, but if not, revocation is effective the first of the following tax year unless made effective in the first 15 days of tax year, in which case it relates back to the beginning of the tax year

b. S corporation status is terminated on the day a terminating event occurs

1.) A terminating event is any event that causes the S corporation to no longer meet the requirements of S corporation status

2.) If a corporation has accumulated earnings and profits as well as passive investment income that exceeds 25% of gross receipts for three consecutive years, its election will be terminated beginning with the following year

c. Taxation at liquidation

1.) S corporations are subject to many of the same liquidation rules applicable to C corporations

2.) In general, the distribution of property to the shareholders in complete liquidation is treated as if the property were sold to the shareholders

3.) The S corporation incurs no tax on liquidation gains

H. LIMITED LIABILITY COMPANIES (LLCs)

1. An LLC provides limited liability to its members and allows great flexibility regarding the taxation of the entity

2. Formation of LLCs

a. To form a new LLC, the members file an article of organization with the state

1.) Costs of forming an LLC may be higher than with other business entities because LLCs are relatively new and there is unfamiliarity

2.) Operating agreement is created

b. A partnership or corporation can be converted to an LLC

c. No limit on the number of members

d. The formation of an LLC is a nontaxable event

3. Taxation of LLCs

a. An LLC can be taxed as any of the following:

1.) Sole proprietorship—only available for single-owner LLCs

a.) The owner will disregard the LLC for tax purposes and simply file a Schedule C on the individual return (Form 1040) to report the activity of the LLC

2.) Partnership—available for LLCs with two or more owners (members)

a.) A partnership return (Form 1065) will be filed to report the income of the LLC

b.) The members will each receive a Schedule K-1 with their apportioned income and will report this income on the appropriate schedule on their individual federal income tax returns (Form 1040)

3.) Corporation—available for any LLC

a.) A corporate return (Form 1120) will be filed to report income of the LLC

b.) Similar to a corporation, the LLC will have two levels of taxation

XXIII. TAXATION OF TRUSTS AND ESTATES

A. IN GENERAL

1. A trust is a legal arrangement whereby an individual transfers legal ownership of property to a trustee
2. Trust income can be taxed to the following
   a. Trust—if income is accumulated in the trust
   b. Beneficiary—if income is distributed from the trust
   c. Grantor—if the trust is a grantor trust (discussed in the following)
3. An estate is a legal entity that comes into existence upon the death of an individual and remains in existence until the decedent's assets pass to the heirs
   a. The estate consists of the probate estate
   b. The estate holds and protects the assets, collects income from those assets, and satisfies obligations of the estate until all the assets are distributed
4. Persons or entities that are responsible for trusts and estates are referred to as fiduciaries

B. TYPES OF TRUSTS

1. Simple trust
   a. Required to distribute all income to beneficiaries each year
   b. Charitable donations are prohibited
   c. Principal distributions are prohibited
2. Complex trust
   a. A trust in which income can be accumulated
   b. Principal can be distributed
   c. The trust pays tax on accumulated income
3. Grantor trust
   a. If a trust is a grantor trust, the grantor pays tax on all trust income
   b. Trust is ignored for income tax purposes
   c. A trust will be a grantor trust if the grantor retains the power to control enjoyment. These powers include the power to:
      1.) add or remove beneficiaries;
      2.) determine the timing of distributions;
      3.) alter the beneficiaries' share of principal or income;
      4.) retain a reversionary interest in either corpus or income;
      5.) control the beneficial enjoyment (either the grantor, a nonadverse party, or both);

6.) retain certain administrative powers;

7.) revoke the trust; and

8.) retain the ability to take income distributions, hold or accumulate income for future distributions to the owner or nonadverse party, or apply income to the payment of life insurance policies on the life of the grantor or the grantor's spouse (e.g., a funded ILIT)

C. FIDUCIARY ACCOUNTING INCOME

1. The accounting income of a fiduciary is determined by the decedent's will (in the case of an estate) or the trust instrument (in the case of a trust)
2. Every fiduciary may have its own unique set of rules for computing accounting income
3. A common difference between fiduciary accounting income and fiduciary taxable income is the treatment of capital gains
    a. For accounting purposes, capital gains generally represent an increase in the value of the principal and are not available for distribution to the income beneficiaries
    b. For tax purposes, the capital gains represent taxable income
4. Trustee fees are generally deductible for tax purposes but may be treated as either income or principal for trust accounting purposes

D. FIDUCIARY TAXABLE INCOME AND DISTRIBUTION DEDUCTION

1. The taxable income of a trust is similar to the calculation of taxable income for an individual taxpayer
2. Major differences between trust taxable income and individual taxable income
    a. A trust is entitled to a deduction for distributions made to beneficiaries
    b. A trust is not entitled to a standard deduction
    c. A trust is entitled to a personal exemption of $300 for a simple trust and $100 for a complex trust
3. If an administrative expense is claimed as a deduction on the estate tax return of a decedent, it may not also be claimed as a deduction on the income tax return of the decedent's estate
    a. The deduction may be prorated between the two returns
4. Medical expenses paid for the care of the decedent before death
    a. If paid within one year after death, medical expenses can be deducted either on the decedent's final income tax return (Form 1040) or the decedent's estate tax return (Form 706), but not both
    b. If paid more than one year after death, expenses can only be deducted on the estate tax return

5. Deduction for distributions made to beneficiaries
   a. The fiduciary is allowed a deduction for the amount of distributions made to beneficiaries during the year
   b. The amount deductible by the fiduciary is the same amount that is taxable to the beneficiaries
   c. The distribution deduction is calculated as the lesser of distributable net income (DNI) or the amount actually distributed to the beneficiaries
   d. Distributable net income (DNI)
      1.) DNI is similar to fiduciary accounting income
      2.) Includes most normal income/expense items
      3.) Excludes items relating to corpus, such as capital gains, stock splits, and depreciation of business assets

E. FIDUCIARY TAX RATES AND FILING REQUIREMENTS

1. Fiduciaries file Form 1041 on or before the 15th day of the fourth month after the close of the tax year. Grantor trusts may also file a Form 1041.
2. A trust must adopt a calendar year
3. Estates may adopt either a calendar year or fiscal year. The first taxable year begins on the day following the decedent's death.
4. Estates and trusts are subject to the following rate schedule (a highly progressive structure)

Estates and Trusts

If taxable income is:	But not over:	The tax rate is:	Of the amount over:
$ 0	$ 2,300	---------------15%	$ 0
$ 2,300	$ 5,450	28%	$ 2,300
$ 5,450	$ 8,300	31%	$ 5,450
$ 8,300	$11,350	36%	$ 8,300
$11,350	---------	39.6%	$11,350

5. Any component of fiduciary taxable income consisting of long-term capital gain is taxed at a maximum rate of 20%
6. Trusts may be subject to alternative minimum tax

F. TAX TREATMENT OF DISTRIBUTIONS TO BENEFICIARIES

1. Beneficiary is taxed on an amount equal to the distribution deduction
2. The fiduciary receives a deduction for the distribution
3. Income distributed to the beneficiary maintains its character (e.g., capital gain, ordinary income, etc.)

4. A beneficiary who receives a distribution from a fiduciary will receive a Schedule K-1 each year
    a. K-1 summarizes the amounts and character of the various items of income that constitute the taxable portion of the distribution
    b. A beneficiary who receives a distribution from a fiduciary with both taxable and nontaxable DNI will only be taxed on a portion of the distribution received

> **EXAMPLE** ABC Trust has DNI of $100,000, of which $40,000 is nontaxable. The beneficiary received a distribution of $20,000 during the year. The distribution received will be taxable in the amount of $12,000 [$20,000 distribution × ($60,000 taxable DNI ÷ $100,000 total DNI)] and nontaxable for the remaining $8,000.

5. Because a simple trust is required to distribute all trust income to its beneficiaries, the entire amount of taxable DNI will be taxed to the beneficiaries each year

XXIV. AUDIT, PENALTIES, AND TAXPAYER'S RIGHTS

A. IN GENERAL

1. The Taxpayer Compliance Measurement Program (TCMP) randomly selected returns used for statistical purposes by the IRS to develop discriminant analysis standards (indefinitely suspended)
2. Audit probability varies with income level and type of income
3. Situations that might trigger an audit
   a. Significant investment losses
   b. Business expenses that produce significant losses
   c. Operating a cash business
   d. Deductions that are larger than the average deductions taken by taxpayers at similar income levels

B. TYPES OF AUDITS

1. A correspondence audit is one in which the issue is generally minor and is performed through the mail
2. An office audit is usually restricted in scope to specific item(s) and is performed at the IRS office
3. A field audit is an examination of numerous items and is performed on the premises of the taxpayer

C. STATUTE OF LIMITATIONS

1. Three years from the filing date of the return or due date if later
2. Six years if 25% of gross income is unreported
3. No statute of limitations for failure to file or if a fraudulent return is filed

D. INTEREST AND PENALTIES

1. Interest—interest runs from unextended due date
2. Penalties
   a. Failure to file: 5% per month, up to a total of 25% (or five months of penalties)
      1.) If the return is filed more than 60 days after the due date or extended due date, the minimum penalty is the smaller of $135 or 100% of the unpaid tax
      2.) A failure-to-file penalty will not be assessed if the taxpayer can show that there was reasonable cause for the failure to file on time
      3.) If failure-to-file penalty is for a fraudulent return, the penalty is increased to 15% per month, up to a total of 75%

b. Failure to pay: .5% per month, up to a total of 25%

1.) If both a failure-to-file penalty and a failure-to-pay penalty apply, the failure-to-file penalty is reduced by the failure-to-pay penalty

c. Accuracy-related penalty—20% of underpayment for intentional disregard of rules and regulations without intent to defraud

> **EXAMPLE** Taxpayer files a timely tax return but fails to pay $15,000 in additional tax of which $6,000 is attributable to the taxpayer's negligence. The negligence penalty will be $1,200 (20% penalty is applied to the $6,000).

d. There are various fraud penalties for deliberate actions (deceit, misrepresentation, and concealment)

> **EXAMPLE** A taxpayer files his tax return 39 days after the due date. Along with the return, he remits a check for $6,000, which is the balance of the tax owed. Disregarding any interest element, the total failure-to-file and failure-to-pay penalties are $600, calculated as follows:
>
> Failure-to-pay penalty:

[½% × $6,000 × 2 (two months; any fraction counts as a full month)]		$60
Plus failure-to-file penalty (5% × $6,000 × 2 months)	$600	
Less failure-to-pay penalty (they run concurrently)	(60)	540
Total penalties (failure-to-file and failure-to-pay)		$600

> The failure-to-file penalty of $600 is reduced by the failure-to-pay penalty of $60, making the adjusted failure-to-file penalty $540. Adding the failure-to-pay penalty of $60 (it reduced but did not eliminate the failure-to-file) results in a total penalty of $600.

E. BURDEN OF PROOF

1. The IRS has the burden of proof on factual matters if the taxpayer has creditable evidence supporting the position

a. The taxpayer must have records and must cooperate with the IRS

b. Corporations, trusts, and estates must have a net worth of $7 million or less to qualify; if they don't qualify, the burden of proof lies with the entity

F. INNOCENT SPOUSE RELIEF

1. If a married couple files jointly, both spouses are jointly and individually responsible for the tax and any interest or penalty due on the joint return

a. One spouse may be held responsible for all the tax due even if all the income was earned by the other spouse

b. However, a spouse may be relieved of the tax, interest, and penalties on a joint tax return in some cases

2. To receive relief, an individual must file Form 8857, Request for Innocent Spouse Relief
   a. An individual should file Form 8857 as soon as he becomes aware of a tax liability for which he believes only his spouse should be held liable
   b. An executor may also file Form 8857 on behalf of a decedent, provided the decedent satisfied the eligibility requirements while alive
3. Types of relief available
   a. Innocent spouse relief
      1.) By requesting innocent spouse relief, an individual can be relieved of responsibility for paying tax, interest, and penalties if his current or former spouse improperly reported (or omitted) items from the joint tax return
      2.) An individual must meet all of the following conditions to qualify for innocent spouse relief
         a.) An individual filed a joint return that has an understatement of tax due as a result of erroneous items (e.g., unreported income and erroneous deductions) of the individual's current or former spouse
         b.) The individual can establish that, at the time he signed the joint return, he did not know and had no reason to know of the understatement of tax
         c.) After taking into account all of the facts and circumstances, it would be unfair to hold the individual liable for the understatement of tax
   b. Relief by separation of liability
      1.) When requesting relief by separation of liability, an individual can allocate any understatement of tax between himself and his spouse
      2.) The individual is responsible for only his own portion of any underpayment
      3.) An individual must meet both of the following conditions to qualify for relief by separation of liability
         a.) The individual must have filed a joint return
         b.) The individual must meet one of the following requirements:
            - The individual is no longer married to (or is separated from) the spouse with whom he filed the joint return
            - The individual was not a member of the same household as the spouse with whom he filed the joint return
   c. Equitable relief
      1.) If an individual does not qualify for innocent spouse relief or relief by separation of liability, he can still be relieved of responsibility for tax, interest, and penalties through equitable relief
      2.) An individual must meet all of the following conditions to qualify for equitable relief:
         a.) The individual does not qualify for innocent spouse relief or relief by separation of liability

b.) The individual and the spouse (or former spouse) did not transfer assets to one another as a part of a fraudulent scheme

c.) The individual did not file the return with the intent to commit fraud

d.) After taking into account all the facts and circumstances, it would be unfair to hold the individual liable for the understatement of tax

e.) The income tax liability from which the individual seeks relief must generally be attributable to an item of the spouse (or former spouse) with whom the individual filed the joint return

G. REPRESENTING CLIENTS BEFORE THE IRS

1. In general
    a. Only a recognized representative can represent a client before the IRS
    b. A representative can act on the client's behalf at conferences, hearings, or meetings with the IRS
    c. The representative must be granted authority to act on behalf of the client. Authority is granted through a power of attorney.
2. Recognized representative
    a. A recognized representative must file a written declaration with the IRS that states he is qualified and authorized to represent the client
    b. Recognized representatives can include the following:
        1.) Attorneys
        2.) Certified public accountants
        3.) Enrolled agents or enrolled actuaries
        4.) Certain unenrolled individuals, such as an unenrolled tax return preparer
            a.) Unenrolled individuals typically have limited authority to represent the client
            b.) Unenrolled individuals must present satisfactory identification and proof of authority to represent the client
    c. Recognized representatives do not include the following:
        1.) Individuals convicted of a criminal offense
        2.) Individuals under disbarment or suspension from practicing as attorneys, certified public accountants, or actuaries
        3.) Individuals who are suspended from practicing before the IRS
        4.) Officers or employees of the US government or District of Columbia
        5.) Members of Congress, if receiving compensation regarding the IRS issue
        6.) CFP® practitioners

3. Power of attorney
    a. A power of attorney is a written authorization for an individual to act on another's behalf
    b. With a power of attorney, any representative (other than an unenrolled preparer) may usually perform the following acts:
        1.) Represent the client before the IRS
        2.) Record the interview
        3.) Sign on the client's behalf
            a.) Waiver of restriction on assessment or collection of a tax deficiency
            b.) Consent to extend the statutory period for assessment or collection of a tax
            c.) Closing agreement
        4.) Receive (but not cash) a refund check
    c. A representative generally cannot sign a client's income tax return, except as preparer

Appendix 1: CFP Board-Provided Handouts

(The formula sheet below was current at press time. Please refer to **http://www.cfp.net/Upload/Publications/170.pdf** for any subsequent updates to the formula sheet.)

CERTIFIED FINANCIAL PLANNER
BOARD OF STANDARDS, INC.

Provided Formulas

These formulas are provided with the exam booklets when taking the CFP® Certification Examination:

$$V = \frac{D_1}{r-g}$$

$$r_i = r_f + (r_m - r_f)\beta_i$$

$$r = \frac{D_1}{P} + g$$

$$r_p = r_f + \sigma_p\left(\frac{r_m - r_f}{\sigma_m}\right)$$

$$COV_{ij} = \rho_{ij}\sigma_i\sigma_j$$

$$S_p = \frac{\overline{r_p} - \overline{r_f}}{\sigma_p}$$

$$\sigma_p = \sqrt{W_i^2\sigma_i^2 + W_j^2\sigma_j^2 + 2W_iW_jCOV_{ij}}$$

$$\alpha_p = \overline{r_p} - \left[\overline{r_f} + \left(\overline{r_m} - \overline{r_f}\right)\beta_p\right]$$

$$\beta_i = \frac{COV_{im}}{\sigma_m^2} = \frac{\rho_{im}\sigma_i}{\sigma_m}$$

$$T_p = \frac{\overline{r_p} - \overline{r_f}}{\beta_p}$$

$$\sigma_r = \sqrt{\frac{\sum_{t=1}^{n}(r_t - \bar{r})^2}{n}}$$

$$D = \frac{\sum_{t=1}^{n}\frac{c_t(t)}{(1+i)^t}}{\sum_{t=1}^{n}\frac{c_t}{(1+i)^t}}$$

$$S_r = \sqrt{\frac{\sum_{t=1}^{n}(r_t - \bar{r})^2}{n-1}}$$

$$D = \frac{1+y}{y} - \frac{(1+y)+t(c-y)}{c\left[(1+y)^t - 1\right]+y}$$

$$CV = \frac{Par}{CP} \times P_s$$

$$\frac{\Delta P}{P} = -D\left[\frac{\Delta y}{1+y}\right]$$

$$IR = \frac{R_P - R_B}{\sigma_A}$$

CFP® | CERTIFIED FINANCIAL PLANNER™ | CFP®

Rev. 12/07

The tax tables provided by CFP Board for the 2011 examinations were unavailable at press time. Please refer to **http://www.cfp.net/become/taxtables.asp** for the tax tables for the 2011 exam cycles.

Appendix 2: How to Prove Certain Business Expenses

IF you have expenses for:	THEN you must keep records that show details of the following elements.			
	Amount	**Time**	**Place or Description**	**Business Purpose and Business Relationship**
Travel	Cost of each separate expense for travel, lodging, and meals. Incidental expenses may be totaled in reasonable categories such as taxis and daily meals for traveler.	Dates you left and returned for each trip and number of days spent on business.	Destination or area of your travel (name of city, town, or other designation).	Purpose: Business purpose for the expense or the business benefit gained or expected to be gained. Relationship: N/A
Entertainment	Cost of each separate expense. Incidental expenses such as taxis and telephones may be totaled on a daily basis.	Date of entertainment. (Also see Business Purpose.)	Name and address or location of place of entertainment. Type of entertainment if not otherwise apparent. (Also see Business Purpose.)	Purpose: Business purpose for the expense or the business benefit gained or expected to be gained. For entertainment, the nature of the business discussion or activity. If the entertainment was directly before or after a business discussion, the date, place, nature, and duration of the business discussion and the identities of the persons who took part in both the business discussion and the entertainment activity. Relationship: Occupations or other information (such as names, titles, or other designations) about the recipients that shows their business relationship to you. For entertainment, you must also prove that you or your employee was present if the entertainment was a business meal.
Gifts	Cost of the gift.	Date of the gift.	Description of the gift.	
Transportation	Cost of each separate expense. For car expenses, the cost of the car and any improvements, the date you started using it for business, the mileage for each business use, and the total miles for the year.	Date of the expense. For car expenses, the date of the use of the car.	Your business destination.	Purpose: Business purpose for the expense. Relationship: N/A

IRS Publication 17; Table 26-2

NOTE: This chart is provided for your convenience as the exam is unlikely to test the substantiation requirements in detail.

Appendix 3:
Reporting Travel, Entertainment, Gift, and Car Expenses and Reimbursements

IF the type of reimbursement (or other expense allowance) arrangement is under:	THEN the employer reports on form W-2:	AND the Employee reports on Form 2106:*
An accountable plan with:		
Actual expense reimbursement: Adequate accounting made and excess returned.	No amount.	No amount.
Actual expense reimbursement: Adequate accounting and return of excess both required but excess not returned.	The excess reported as wages in box 1.	No amount.
Per diem or mileage allowance (up to federal rate): Adequate accounting and excess returned.	No amount.	All expenses and reimbursements only if excess expenses are claimed. Otherwise, form is not filed.
Per diem or mileage allowance (exceeds federal rate): Adequate accounting up to the federal rate only and excess not returned.	The excess amount as wages in box 1. The amount up to the federal rate is reported only in box 12—it is not reported in box 1.	All expenses (and reimbursement reported on Form W-2, box 12) only if expenses in excess of the federal rate are claimed. Otherwise, form is not required.
A nonaccountable plan with:		
Either adequate accounting or return of excess, or both, not required by plan.	The entire amount is reported as wages in box 1.	All expenses.
No reimbursement plan:	The entire amount as wages in box 1.	All expenses.
* You may be able to use Form 2106-EZ. See Completing Forms 2106 and 2106-EZ.		

IRS Publication 17, Table 26-3

Appendix 4:
Are My Points Fully Deductible This Year?

Publication 17; Figure 23-B

NOTE: It is unlikely that this detail will be tested on the exam. The chart is provided for your convenience.

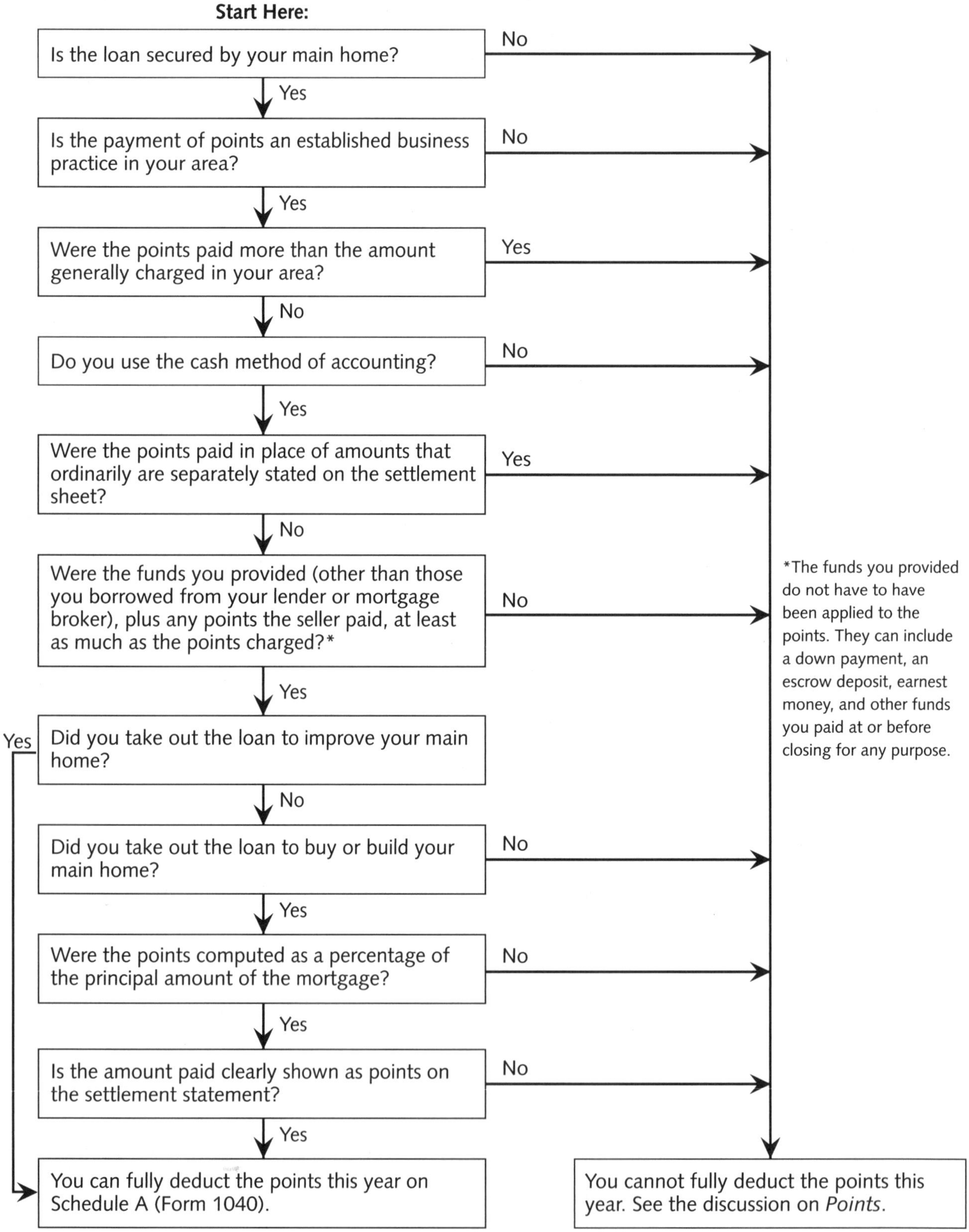

Index

A

B

C

P

Q

R

S

Notes

Notes

Notes

Notes

Notes

Notes

Notes

Notes